BEST
CREATIVE NONFICTION
OF THE SOUTH

Volume I:
Virginia

BEST
CREATIVE NONFICTION
OF THE SOUTH

VOLUME I:
VIRGINIA

Casey Clabough and Thorpe Moeckel, Editors

Texas Review Press
Huntsville, Texas

Requests for permission to acknowledge material from this work should be
sent to:

Permissions
Texas Review Press
English Department
Sam Houston State University
Huntsville, TX 77341-2146

ACKNOWLEDGEMENTS:

Many thanks to the writers and publishers who made the ensuing work available for inclusion in this collection. Their participation and generosity, along with the exceptional support of Paul Ruffin and Texas Review Press, have made this series possible. Beyond the availability of the content itself, a great many minds and hands conspired to bring the collection together, including students Julianna Fialkowski, Erin Gough, and Martha Park.

Cover design by Nancy Parsons, Graphic Design Group

Library of Congress Cataloging-in-Publication Data

Names: Clabough, Casey, 1974- editor. | Moeckel, Thorpe, editor.
Title: Best creative nonfiction of the South / [edited by] Casey Clabough,
    Thorpe Moeckel.
Description: Huntsville, Texas : Texas Review Press, [2016]-
Identifiers: LCCN 2015047566 (print) | LCCN 2015050241 (ebook) |
ISBN
    9781680030754 (pbk. : alk. paper) | ISBN 9781680030761 (e-book)
Subjects: LCSH: Creative nonfiction, American--Southern States.
 Creative
    nonfiction, American--21st century. | LCGFT: Creative nonfiction.
Classification: LCC PS659.2 .B485 2016 (print) | LCC PS659.2
(ebook) | DDC
    810.8/0975--dc23
LC record available at http://lccn.loc.gov/2015047566

Contents

Permissions

Series Statement

The series editor and the publisher of *Best Creative Nonfiction of the South* created this state-by-state series of volumes in order to gather together the best creative nonfiction of living Southern writers organized by the states from which they hail or in which they actively have lived for several decades. Creative nonfiction has various definitions but typically encompasses such forms of writing as the personal essay, literary journalism, memoir, and travel writing. It often is described as true stories which are rendered using the tools and craft of fiction.

Best Creative Nonfiction of the South serves as a valuable resource for scholars, students, writers, and general readers interested in creative nonfiction both from specific areas of the South and across the region as a whole. The writers included in each volume come from diverse backgrounds, generations, and artistic traditions. Most, if not all, volumes in the series indirectly reflect literary changes over time and/or how literary variations have manifested themselves in a given state. In some cases, publisher permissions and other factors have prevented the editors from including the work of deserving writers. Nevertheless, the abundant literary talent across the South has lessened the impact of the occasional unfortunate omission.

The various states of the South keep evolving, as do their cultures and arts. *The Best Creative Nonfiction of the South* series offers provocative glimpses both of Southern literary tradition and change in the twenty-first century.

—Casey Clabough, Series Editor

BEST
CREATIVE NONFICTION
OF THE SOUTH

VOLUME I:

VIRGINIA

Adrian Blevins

Late-Breaking Yew Berry News from the Madman's Love Shack

The catalogue of infractions I have committed against this world would flood a small library, for what it's worth. I pilfered a pack of gum before I could talk and pretended to know how to write in cursive at the age of five. When I showed my cousin the hieroglyphics I'd scratched all over her Scooby Doo drawing pad, I furthermore felt something like pride as she broke down in tears and went running to her mom because she couldn't even write in regular letters yet. I distinctly remember cheating on a philosophy exam when I was in college; the plan took at least a week's work of pre-meditation and is therefore fused into my memory like the three times I gave birth without so much as a shot of whisky. Speaking of whisky, I drove drunk more times than I can remember during my pre-maternal years and smoked pot when I was pregnant after they'd commenced. I let my kids skip school to keep me company when I was lonely. I also put them into bed with me when I felt desolate and told them to go back to sleep when they claimed to be thirsty. Oh, yes, I called in sick when I wasn't sick. Oh yes, I talked about myself for an hour and half when I was supposed to be teaching my students how to recognize a sentence fragment.

As for how klutzy I am—as for how often I fall trying to walk up a flight of stairs or knock a door I'm opening into my own forehead—as for my inability to understand geography and history and physics and anything else that is by design complicated and mathematical and boring—this is already a part of the public record. I remember believing my father when he told me that the cows in the fields on the way to my grandmother's farm were statues—never mind that I could watch them lie down, eat, and open their mouths to moo. I remember saying I'd never drive a car, get divorced, smoke a cigarette, or put my tongue in a man's mouth and wiggle it around. Of course I've done all these things and worse, falling down on the way and bruising my hips, lips, and pride as though I was born to be a clown and not a mother or a fidgety writer.

But the only infractions that really bother me are the ones I've committed against myself. Thus this long prelude in which I admit to being mean and dim-witted is just a kind of curtain behind which I am going to hide, for the infraction against myself I most don't want to confess concerns a she that could not make out the forest from the trees. It concerns a recently-divorced she bent on vengeance, a single-mom she who'd spent her entire life learning how to rationalize the unsound, the unwise, and the unfounded by reading *Wuthering Heights* and *Gone With the Wind* thirty-seven and one-half times. This writer she is so obsessive she only took English electives in college and graduate school and therefore didn't have time for Psychology 101. In Psychology 101 the professors are bound to spend a week teaching students how to recognize a madman. In Psychology 101 the professors are bound to stand up behind their podiums and describe the enemy. If they don't, they should. If they don't, they are themselves the enemy.

The madman said he loved me on the bank of a clichéd river. We were drinking a bottle of clichéd wine. The clichéd river and the clichéd wine filled me up with the foetid venom of the hot-pink yew-berry. I mean, the clichéd river and the clichéd wine caused the universe to rupture, since I said something like, "yes, yes, I love you too," though he was quite possibly the most loathsome man in America. Nevertheless I was single for the first time since I'd turned eighteen.

Nevertheless it was dusk—the time of day in that poem by James Wright in which twilight "bounds softly forth on the grass." Steam was rising from the rippling water, birds were cawing overhead, and I am certain there had to be fish somewhere, opening and closing their ravenous mouths. The water and the birds made me feel like a contemporary Venus on a Halfshell or some-goddess-else out of a good painter's dreamy imagination. I was a modern Mona Lisa; I was one of Gauguin's naked tribal girls; I was Madonna in black lace licking a half-baked thing off her foolish pinkie finger.

He lived in a love shack in the woods when the weather was warm enough. I call this mongoose hole a love shack because love is what he pretended to feel whenever he was there. It was really a two-room LSD getaway that his stepfather left behind when he ran off to drown at sea. Pretending love was exciting at first, with the owls in the trees hooting their midnight elegies and the raccoon babies under the porch sniffing around for tossed-out celery sticks. Pretending love in the love shack even seemed romantic, at first. I could think of him as a new-fangled Thoreau simplifying his life for the sake of the nation. I'd even go home and read Thoreau for encouragement after a love shack visit: Thoreau said, "all good things are wild and free," I'd write in my journal. I'd then tell my mother that my new boyfriend was an aesthete, a hermit-philosopher, a spirit-man like Joseph Campbell or Robert Bly. My mother, being wise, would sigh.

But the love shack didn't even have an outhouse. Or what outhouse there had been was now overgrown with vines and crawling with snakes and spiders. This meant that we had to go to his mother's house to use the bathroom. There wasn't even a kitchen in the love shack. Well, there once had been a kitchen, but it was filled with trash, so he kept blocks of cheese in the creek and ate these with crackers or obscenely long loaves of bread, pretending to be French. He also kept six-packs of beer in the creek and the bottles of wine I'd bring over when

3

my children were spending the weekend with their father. I wanted him to clean up the love shack and the outhouse, of course—I wanted him to cut out a big circle around the outhouse with the scythe he didn't own and cover the walls inside with poems by James Wright and paintings of Italian people eating grapes. I wanted him to burn the love shack, really. I wanted him to get a job and leave his mother and write a book or at least buy a truck with valves that didn't knock. But he was too busy sleeping, which was perhaps the first sign that Eden was not Eden and he not Adam and she—she not Eve.

He was in his late thirties, returning to college to study English Literature after many years of doing semi-religious things that I never did understand. He was tall, good-looking, articulate, and chronically unemployed. The fact that he was a college student helped account for his housing and money trouble, or so I told myself during this yewberry state. I thought college was a good idea, since his limited work history included lifting heavy boxes for UPS and washing off dead people in a variety of West Virginian funeral homes, but he could only study for about an hour before he'd have to take a nap. Once, toward the end of the nine months we spent together, he took me to visit his sister, who was married to a halfway famous rock star, which was supposed to impress me. He pulled over on the side of the road in some residential neighborhood a couple of miles from his sister's house. I thought at first that he wanted to make out, which seemed odd in its timing and unwise in its setting. Instead he pulled his cap over his head and said in this prissy, British tone that he liked to affect, "let us take a little nap."

There were children outside playing on their bikes or tossing basketballs into hoops that had no nets—there were people everywhere mowing lawns and women in housedresses watering ferns—and still he pushed the driver's seat as far back as it would go and spread out his legs. I sat there and looked at him and sighed. I stared at the knobs on the radio and at the light blue upholstery in my Toyota. I pondered our cooler of beer in the back seat. I looked outside at the sunshine filtering down through the trees like bleached little hemp ropes and sighed even more. Maybe I started a fight—maybe I said, "you're crazy, something's wrong with you." Maybe I went back through my mind to the texts I'd begun to gather on depression and neurosis and told myself how much I hated Sylvia Plath and Ann Sexton for being insane and making me think I had to be crazy and date crazy men to prove it; maybe I leaned back in the car and closed my own eyes. Probably I just sat there; probably I thought of a poem against him and promised myself I'd write it all down when I got home, which probably I didn't.

If he wasn't sleeping, he was reading Milton out loud on the double bed with the confederate flag bedspread. I'm a poet, and still I couldn't stand him reading Milton. Sometimes, reading Milton, he'd cry. I'd listen out of writerly admiration for the vast scope and breadth of his feeling for the English language, which I took to represent the vast scope and breadth of his crazy man's heart. If he wasn't reading Milton, he was singing Irish ballads about girls dying and coming back and walking along the Cliffs of Moor in billowing black capes. If he wasn't singing Irish songs, he was talking about how the Jews ran everything in America; if I said he was being anti-Semitic and stupid and hateful he'd give me a lecture on how materialistic and uninformed I was. I'd tell him about Marina Tsvetaeva, the Russian poet, saying "all poets are Jews," and he'd say all poets were Irish. As if to prove him right, I'd get out of bed and find a drink. I'd scrub something—I'd go outside and stand under the big oak tree and pray to God to give me a way out that wouldn't get anybody killed. I'd tell him I should see other men. Of course, I'd only do this when I was very drunk. He'd try to kick me out of the love shack. I'd say, "well, I'm too drunk to drive right now, but the minute I get sober, I'm going." He would say, "you don't mean it," and I'd insist I did. He would get his keys to the knocking truck and start to walk down the hill. I'd suddenly be afraid to spend the night alone in the love shack since a boy had been killed near it not a year earlier. I'd wonder if he'd been the killer; I'd shiver; I'd cross my chest like I was a Catholic and not an atheist; I'd scream his name and follow him down the path that led to the road, saying, "you need to see a doctor."

The doctors said he was depressed, potentially psychotic, and an alcoholic. I took him several times to several hospitals—I stood there beside him and signed papers that said I'd be responsible for him and nodded my head and feigned concern, though what I really felt was fear that he would kill me or himself if I left him. He'd promise to stop drinking and take his Prozac. But he couldn't stop drinking, and the Prozac interfered with the operations of his penis, which already had issues on account of the alcohol.

I knew in those days of an ex-nun who was also an ex-alcoholic. She talked of spiritual things the way he did—they both acted as though they had the answers to every mystery from albino dogs to the kinds of clothes Jesus wore. I told myself that it might make good sense to introduce them, since I wasn't doing anything for him but becoming an alcoholic myself and he wasn't doing anything for me but driving me mad. Maybe I had it in my mind then that he would really like her; maybe I was trying to find a way to make him stop drinking. In any case, one night we went to my friend the ex-nun's house. She made spaghetti and they talked of the scriptures—of New York and the scriptures—of AA and New York and the scriptures—while I sat at the kitchen table and pretended the plastic spoon on the table was a top, spinning it around and around until I got dizzy and went home alone and threw up.

The next weekend my kids weren't home I cleaned out his kitchen with Ajax and a stainless steel brush; I took the bags of trash to the dump and bleached his sink and sewed curtains and placed a new broom in the corner of the room. I bought dishes, hand towels, and a small refrigerator. I dusted and vacuumed the walls of the love shack;

I rearranged the furniture and picked up the trash in the yard and brought a couple of rocking chairs from my house and sat them side-by-side on the love shack's front porch. I bought him *On Suicide*, four shirts, and books about writing. I put his tapes of Irish drinking songs into alphabetical order on the bookshelf and tied the love letters of old girlfriends together with a piece of red ribbon and laid them with matchbooks and new pens into a little Easter basket, which I placed in the center of the coffee table. I stacked his wood for the woodstove up in a pile and covered it with plastic wrap. Meanwhile he went to his classes and slept in the hammock in the yard. Meanwhile he drank cheap beer and got a black cat and named her Prozac and read Milton by the big oak tree and called my friend the ex-nun on the phone and told her he was in love with her.

He may have even said she was the love of his life. Certainly he spat his well-rehearsed come-on all over the phone while sipping a clear bottle of something and wiping the residue of it off his mouth with the back of this hand. I don't know for sure, though, and I don't want to. I've heard from other friends that the ex-nun may have visited the madman's love shack a couple of times, and God forgive her. God forgive each of us these yew berry transgressions, I mean in conclusion to say: God forgive us for being needy and selfish and unreasonably optimistic about the gone-astray. God forgive us for scrubbing the filthy world until our hands turn pink. Finally our eyes do blink open: we spit out the yew-berry, open the doors to our Toyotas, and drive on home to our kids. They'll be carving jack-o-lanterns at the kitchen table. They'll have four or five already lit with candles. Thus that buoyant scent of pumpkins—I'm not lying—hanging triumphant in the autumn air.

Greg Bottoms

Black Preacher at the Family Reunion

In 1982, the year you were eleven, your dad's family reunion was held at a public park in Newport News, Virginia. It was a place of woods and creeks and picnic tables, set against the eastern shore of the southern part of the James River, a few miles before it empties into the Chesapeake Bay. You heard more than one family member that day say they hoped the place wouldn't get *overrun by the locals*, meaning the packs of young black males on bikes or on foot from the surrounding poor neighborhoods. They were often there playing basketball on the cracked and faded courts.

You and several of your male cousins—four or five boys, you will remember—played war in the woods while you waited to be called to the picnic area for lunch, where fifty or so relatives, toddlers to the elderly, would chattily swarm around the splintered tables and pile their flimsy paper plates with fried chicken and salads from KFC, and all manner of cover-dish appetizers and desserts—soft-shell crabs, coleslaw, banana pudding, lemon squares.

After playing for an hour or so in the woods, one of your older cousins, Kevin, a chubby fourteen-year-old with a mean, crooked-toothed grin and a mom-inflicted haircut, dared you to yell *nigger* at the basketball players from behind a thick copse of trees. You were looking out at a full court of ten older black boys and young men, most maybe sixteen to twenty years old, muscles and sweat and back-and-forth joking. One older man—he looked about thirty-five—wore athletic glasses with a band holding them onto his head. You thought he was a teacher, maybe a coach, because everyone listened to him; they waited to see what he would say when there was a foul, a potential foul. He was the center of their disbanding and reforming circles on the court.

You stared at the men and boys, especially at the man you thought a teacher, who came across as a person of real dignity and authority, and then at the metal hoops and backboards, the falling-down fencing, rolled up in places like the edges of once-wet paper. The backboards looked indestructible, like big, square storm grates, and you had been told, had heard, many times, that that was because blacks (what a strange descriptor, you thought even then, for people with skin of widely varying shades of brown) would steal anything they could carry, even a heavy backboard. When you were very young, because of things white people (who are actually more pink or tan or beige) told you, and because you were a child and when you are a child everything said is the truth, there is no such thing as a word that is not the truth—because why would there be?— you imagined the houses of black people were filled with pointless objects, stolen for the sake of stealing. Almost every word out of every mouth that you understood to be trustworthy made you believe that black people operated like rats, running wild in the secret streets, hording the unusable. They were incoherent, savage. And they couldn't swim.

I'm not going to do that, you said to Kevin, hiding from the court now in the deep-green foliage, sweating in the heat, the wet sunshine, sweating from running and climbing the small hills, hills where Revolutionary War soldiers and Confederate and Union soldiers had walked and climbed and run and screamed and fought and killed and died. Sometimes you felt the layers of time beneath your feet—or that is how you will remember it. Smell of honeysuckle. Saw of bees. Penny-colored pine needles. Stripe of gold light stenciled onto green grass. Earth smell so strong it must have come from inside your own head. Virginia. Childhood. You grow old.

You go everywhere in the country, travel the world, and you sit down to write a sentence and you are still there.

Yeah, you are, said Kevin.

No, I'm not, you said, laughing, trying to make it seem as if the whole thing was ridiculous, would require no more of your attention.

Kevin took out a knife, a little plastic knife from KFC, serrated on one side, translucent and blue-tinted, and held it up to your throat as the other cousins stood around watching though you won't actually remember them doing this just remember that they were there and that is what they would do in a scene and this is a story and you are a writer so just go ahead and imagine the other cousins, four of them, ragged white boys with filthy clothes and knees and faces or whatever. Dirt-creased necks, black-edged fingernails. Tap into your repository of working-class white people stereotypes, if you like. Use "trailer park" as a place holder in the draft.

Do it or I'll cut your throat, Kevin said.

You thought about it, yelling the word and then running and it would all really just be a game, some fun at the reunion, but you didn't want to do it because the man, you still believed, was a teacher of some kind, and he was teaching the boys playing and maybe not only basketball but other things, too, because he kept stopping to talk to them and pat them on the back, and they were paying attention and smiling, laughing at what seemed like his jokes.

You felt the cousins holding you and you felt the dull knife edge saw across your neck and you felt—you will feel it again later, remembering—that electric sting, the hot blood on your skin, the panicked slap of your hand on the wound.

And later you showed your mom the cut at lunch but didn't say how it happened and your mom said *what happened, a stick?* and you said, *yeah, a stick*, and then she put a napkin against your neck. She lifted the napkin and looked every couple of minutes until the bleeding stopped, said: *Some stick. Careful.*

Then this image: it was hours later and you

were standing in the parking lot at dusk and the black man with glasses in a sweat-stained gray shirt was laughing with all the other black boys and young men as they loaded their basketballs and bags into a clean, new, white church van that had written on its side the Holy Redeemer something something Church of Christ. You must have been with your mom and dad and brothers but they aren't in the memory. It's just you at the end of a hot day with a raw, pink cut on your neck and dirt-stained everything and the sky is gray-blue with a distended pink belly.

You are staring at the black man and patting gently at your neck. He shuts the van doors. He walks toward you and asks if you are okay and you say *yeah I am except my neck got cut out in the woods* and the black man says he likes to use Bactine on his cuts—you'll remember this very clearly—even though it burns a little at first but the cut goes away faster and that is usually all there is to it. *Good as new. You can get it down at the drug store. Give you some, son, if I had it, but we left the aid kit at church.*

You look at the man. He is smiling. You want to say that you got your throat cut because you wouldn't yell *nigger* at him, but you don't know how. Talking. Other people. You back then. You might as well have been trying to rebuild a car engine, or do particle physics.

Before the man gets in the van and drives away, he says *God bless you, son.* Then he pats you gently on the shoulder and looks into you. A second. Two seconds. Brown eyes and blue eyes. Nothing much. Why even remember this?

But in your dad's '65 Mustang, on the way home, your mom turns around and says *why are you crying what's wrong is something wrong*, and you say *it's my neck, my neck hurts*, and your mom says *we'll take care of it honey we will just calm down*, but it's not your neck, or the anger and shame and helplessness you feel because of your cruel and stupid cousin Kevin, who could have done anything he wanted to you—beaten you delirious, hung you from a tree. You don't know what it is. Exhaustion, the long day, the plastic picnic knife, your white family, those black boys and men, the squalor of the poor neighborhoods near the park turning slowly and darkly now in the car windows, a hand on your shoulder, a blessing at dusk. The world expands every day. Words barely touch it. And now your heart has opened like a sieve and you cannot hold back its tiny flood.

Michael P. Branch

Hillbillicus Virginianus: On the Road with Nature in the Appalachians

Some years ago my friend Dan and I decided that we should make a book about our home: the Blue Ridge Mountains and Shenandoah Valley of Virginia. We had the modest goal of creating an anthology of nature writing from Virginia that would put *our* map on *the* map—a book that would add our beautiful corner of the South to the big map on which New York and Boston figured so prominently. We wanted to sharpen our hickory sabers and storm the cultural establishment from the south—the direction from which a literary assault is least expected. When we finished it six years later, *The Height of Our Mountains* collected, to quote the jacket hype, "the work of seventy of the nation's finest writers on nature since 1607."

If you've ever done a book tour, or known anybody who has, you know that a book tour is the most pathetic form of self-immolation ever born from the dark imagination of humankind. Making a book is like spending years alone, dragging a boulder across a field in the withering sun, and publishing it is like dropping it into a well and waiting indefinitely to hear a splash. But the special perversity of a book tour is that it dramatizes and enacts this brutal splashlessness in the most visceral way possible. Unless you're mighty famous, touring a book is like inviting your whole town over to watch you step in a steel trap and chew your own leg off to escape—and then having only four people show up. Maybe Emily Dickinson had the right idea: work tirelessly on your writing, invest yourself in it completely, then sew it up into neat little bundles, pack it in a trunk, and under no circumstances leave the house.

Ignoring common sense—which, as Mark Twain pointed out, is an odd name for something so uncommon—Dan and I decided we should do a book tour. If we were going to put our home patch of the South on the Literary Map of Empire, we had to get the word out among the ranks. But the problem with making books about your home place is that by the time you finish them you live someplace else. If you're a Virginian you cannot help but wish desperately that you *didn't* live someplace else, and yet you do. Then you have to buy a plane ticket to get back home so you can tell people there about their own place and why they should care deeply about it and take care of it and never leave—and, by the way, how much you miss it since you moved away. So Dan and I each took ten days of vacation from our jobs in other parts of the country and flew home to Virginia. We scraped together some money and rented a bright red car and filled the trunk and back seat with boxes of our book (would these be enough?), and we set out to tour the region represented by the selections included in the book—and to enlist readers to help us show those literary carpetbaggers what real nature writing looks like.

We're now a week into the tour and we've already done more than a dozen gigs. We did a reading at the Virginia State Arboretum near Winchester, a town in which every truckstop and diner has a shrine devoted to Patsy Cline, a poor Winchester girl who made good in the big world beyond the mountains. At that reading seven people showed up, but most had come to look at flowers and wandered in by mistake. And we *almost* did a reading in D.C., where the bookstore had a lovely display of our book behind two little folding chairs. There we sat, in our little chairs, waiting until we were sure nobody was coming. One kid, who addressed me as "Dude," asked where the rack of CliffsNotes was. After a reading at a bookstore in old town Alexandria that evening I had a chance to be avuncular to several of my old friends' children and to play music all night with one of my buddies. In the morning I sat with his kids at the breakfast table, learning about dinosaurs and washing down Cap'n Crunch and aspirin with black coffee.

We've also done a few readings in Charlottesville, where Dan and I first met as graduate students at the University of Virginia. Here I've visited old hangouts, old friends, old trees—even stopped by the statue of The General riding Traveler across the town square. And we've done gigs in a few of the state's many Burgs—Harrisonburg, Lynchburg, Fredericksburg, Blacksburg—and in several small mountain towns where we shall forever remain famous as the only people ever foolish enough to do a public reading. Our gig in the tiny Appalachian hamlet of Luray—a reading with six people in attendance—was held in the sandwich shop on Main Street. And while we're received kindly everywhere we go, this book tour has confirmed for me the existentialist maxim that, to paraphrase, everybody is the hero of their own life story and nobody else really gives a shit. Several readings have been busts, and even those that succeed do so with such spectacular modesty that I can't stop wishing I were fishing instead. In a perverse moment I run the numbers and calculate that, considering the royalties generated by our book sales so far as compared to the hours we've spent on the project over the last six years, we are being compensated at a rate of approximately six pennies per hour.

We've been on the road a solid week now, and today promises to be especially grueling. This will be a long, busy day in which we will do three readings in three different towns. I picture myself looking into the camera on a late-night TV ad as I stand in front of the hotel in the rain, holding our book up carefully, so my fingers won't obscure the cover: "the tour budget is a-kinda small," I say in an exaggerated Piedmont drawl, "but the tour hotel is Econo-lage." The weather has been terrible all week, and I can't eat any more grits. Tour readings have become occasions for me to say things like "a strong, local sense of place is vitally important to the maintenance of a nurturing relationship between human communities and the natural environments that sustain them"—before turning to Dan to whisper, "What the hell town is this, anyway?" I'm stiff as roadkill from all the driving and bad beds and there are still three long days to go.

I check out of the hotel, pausing to jawbone with the desk jockey about capitalism, religion, flooding, monster truck racing, and how to raise kids up right ("spar the rod, sperl the chile," he admonishes me). Promising that I'll go either to church or to the monster truck rally I get directions to the diner and we're off to start our long day. As we roll out I scan the car radio for something to drive by, but radio in this part of the world is limited mostly to fiddle music, preaching, and Lynyrd Skynyrd. On this trip I've been happy to find that when we turn on the radio in the middle of the night anywhere in Virginia I can still identify the general location simply by "FPF": the ratio of fiddling to preaching to "Freebird." It's good to be home.

The first of our three gigs today is an interview and reading on a regional public television show taped in a modest studio in Roanoke. We arrive early and are led to a waiting room, where I wash down my salt bomb breakfast with more bad joe. Soon the host of the show fetches us and leads us into the studio. He isn't a TV person, but rather a person on TV—a real person, with a big belly and a bushy beard. He looks like a professional bass fisherman in a sport coat, about to do a regional-feed, late-night TV endorsement for a spinnerbait—or a mortuary, or an Econo-Lodge. We're shown the studio setup: two cameras, three chairs, and lots of bright lights.

Literary fame at last! The interview and discussion come off smoothly, and even a bellyful of viscous grits and acidic coffee can't ruin what turns out to be a surprisingly good experience. Maybe the secret to our success here is that, for once, we don't have to worry about whether people are going to show up— we can just fantasize that our fellow Virginians are huddled anxiously around their TV sets in order to be enlightened by our work. This is an act of faith much like the leap we have made in imagining an audience for our book, and so it is both a labor of love and a form of self-delusion that we have had six years to perfect.

We talk with the host about our deep love for the great beauty of wild Virginia, and we lament the loss of wildness that our book helps chart. We read a few representative pieces and then time's up. Our fifteen minutes of fame lasts twenty-one, and now it's back to the road. As we're walked to the door Dan asks when the show will air. "Oh, next week. No editing, you know. Got to be next week," says the host. "After that the weather will get good and everybody'll start fishing." The warm glow of the studio lights is already dimming in my mind, and as we run across the muddy parking lot in the rain I find myself wondering what a TV audience no-show would look like. First I picture my beaming face on a television screen in an empty living room; then I picture a living room full of people as one of them clicks the channel from my face to the face of a singing, juggling, unicycle-riding twelve-year-old girl on *America's Got Talent*.

We're back in the car and off to Lexington, the heart of southern culture in Virginia, and the buckle on the Bible Belt if your pants ride as high as some I've seen today. A picturesque, sleepy southern town infused with a subtle sense of superiority, Lexington is home to both the Virginia Military Institute, which not so very long ago was forced by law to accept women students, and the more progressive Washington and Lee University, which went co-ed back in the dark ages of the Reagan era. Arriving in time to plan our reading at W&L, we sit down on a set of worn marble steps in front of a small, lovely church near central campus to work out a series of readings featuring writers from this part of the state. As we talk I watch both VMI and W&L students walking by; it is easy enough to tell them apart, since the VMI cadets are wearing full dress uniforms today. As a group of cadets walks by I notice that all salute in unison as they pass. Another group passes. Again, all salute. Is it possible they've already seen us on TV? Suddenly a number of disparate threads unite in my mind. "Dan . . . this is the General's tomb!" Sure enough, we are sitting next to Lee Chapel, where Robert Edward is resting—or still trying to put the whole thing to rest.

This ritual saluting of the General is the rule rather than the exception in this part of Virginia, where the War Between the States—occasionally referred to locally as the War of Northern Aggression— is still being fought in churches and classrooms and poolhalls and on the walls above urinals. Some folks around here still hold the not-so-crazy view that our nation's best hope was agrarianism and local self-determination and believe that this hope was dashed by the industrial war machine of a government that tyrannized over its people. *Sic Semper Tyrannis* ("Thus Always to Tyrants") is the motto on the Virginia state flag, which not so subtly depicts a tall lady standing on a guy's throat. Any Virginian will tell you that our history is vitally important to us, but we may not tell you that here at home our history is rarely in the past.

At W&L we're received with inimitable southern graciousness. An elegant luncheon is served with crystal, silver, and china on a table set out on the brick verandah of a historical building on campus. This clearly beats the not-so-solid diet of Jack Daniels and Cheez Whiz I've been on in various cheap hotels along our route. Our reading is well attended but, as with most university events other than football games and frat parties, there's a suspiciously high percentage of unwilling conscripts—draftees in the extra credit infantry, easily spotted as they soldier on to keep their eyes open against long odds. As we leave Lexington after the reading I somehow can't shake the feeling that we'll be pulled over and imprisoned by local sheriff's deputies, who will subject us to interrogation about etiquette, genealogy, and Civil War history while depriving us of whiskey. It has been a good stop in the genteel heart of our home state, but now we're off to the hardcore hillbilly haven of southwest Virginia—a country characterized by a disconcertingly high FPF.

The weather, at first awful, turns worse. The creeks are cresting and the hollows have begun to flood. As we approach Martinsville we stop at a roadside store for a cup of anything hot. The place doesn't seem to have a name, though it does have a handpainted sign out front that reads "Amunition and Picknick Supplies." As I walk through the barnboard door I spot a shelf containing moon pies and wonderbread, and then, immediately below, 100-pound bags of Dixie Crystal. When was the last time you stopped by your local convenience store for 100 pounds of sugar? We're now in the leading bootleg liquor producing county in the nation, and the panther's breath still flows out of these copper-coiled hollows five hundred gallons at a time. Virginia is the only state in the Union—well, most of it is in the Union, though I suspect holdouts in this neighborhood—with an interdiction squad dedicated to still-busting. Amazing as it seems, a technologically updated version of the old "revenooer" cat-and-mouse game is still being played in these mountains. I buy some coffee, which is oily, lukewarm, and comes in a partially melted styrofoam cup that looks as if a rodent has chewed its rim. Ignoring the beefsticks, plug tobacco, and rebel flag decals that surround me at the counter, I hustle back out into the storm.
As a Virginian I'm painfully aware that this sort

of characterization reads like cheap—perhaps even traitorous—cliché, but this is exactly the sort of place that spawns the unhandsome southern stereotypes that are perennial in American popular culture. In this part of the state we've exchanged *Gone with the Wind* for *Deliverance*, and I'm feeling a little guilty for wishing I could go back to being *from* Virginia instead of actually being *in* it. We are now deep within the home territory of my old neighbors, the reclusive and occasionally dangerous members of the mountain tribe *Hillbillicus virginianus*. I can't help but recall a spate of recirculating jokes offered at the expense of the region—jokes that fall into three general categories: 1) clannishness, as in "If a southwest Virginia couple gets divorced, are they still brother and sister?"; 2) personal hygiene, as in "Did you know the toothbrush was invented in southwest Virginia—if it had been invented anywhere else it would have been called the teethbrush"; and, 3) socioeconomic status, as in "What do a Florida hurricane and a southwest Virginia divorce have in common? Either way somebody's gonna lose a trailer." They're awful stereotypes, but I can't help wondering what we were thinking when we decided to bring a book tour into a community where less than two percent of folks go to college, only half finish high school, and more people than I can stand to admit can't read at all. But the possibility that heartbreaking illiteracy and poverty rates might have a dampening effect on book sales isn't something our pride and our love of this region allow us to contemplate. And so the red rental car literary medicine show rolls on into the sticks, even as Dan reminds me that the royalties from all the books we've sold so far won't cover the Cheez Whiz—let alone the Old No. 7—that I've consumed along our way.

There are plenty of divorces and trailers around here, and although there are no hurricanes, we do have the next worst thing: tornadoes. The radio reports that forty secondary roads in the county are flooded out, with families trapped up in their hollows until whenever the water recedes. Now even the major roads are mostly impassable. There's a tornado watch for the whole area, and ten minutes later the radio crackles that several twisters have touched down nearby. One hits six miles from where we're supposed to read tonight, and somebody does lose a trailer when a corkscrew blast of wind spreads their doublewide into the pasture.

Tonight's reading is sponsored by a local museum, but their building is under renovation and so we will be presenting at "Shady Meadows," which has been described only as an "alternative venue." It sounds like it ought to be a graveyard. And how can meadows be shady? The whole gig feels shady to me. We follow convoluted directions to Shady Meadows, which, when we finally arrive, turns out to be an old folks home out on the edge of town. I can't help but take stock. Day eight. Gig three of the day. Flooding. Tornadoes. Illiteracy. Too many grits. Hundred-pound bags of Dixie Crystal. Rebel flags everywhere. Old pickups conspicuously without those bumper stickers that read "Southern by the grace of God, liberal by education and choice." Too much fiddling and preaching and not nearly enough "Freebird." Total exhaustion. The potentially catastrophic departure of my sense of humor. All this I can handle, but not a gig in an old folks home—anything but this.

I've got a bad feeling about this one, but how can we possibly back out? I begin to pray for cancellation, for the liberating humiliation of a no-show. We've still got several long days of readings to go, and I already feel as if my neurons have stopped firing. I visualize the headlines in the local paper: "Idealistic Young Scholar Suffocates While Trying to Wedge Pointy Head into Local Community. Funeral to be Held at Shady Meadows." "Dan," I ask through closed jaws, "whose idea was this book tour?"

We stall as long as possible in the car, listening to tinny fiddle music on the radio and gathering our strength. It has been a long trip and a longer day, and I've already reckoned this gig so inauspicious that I am compelled to stop by the trunk for a shot of Jack and a spurt of Whiz in the rain before heading inside. Lugging our albatross box of unsold books into the building, we are escorted to the room where the reading will take place. But our lecture venue, to my deep dismay, is the rest home's chapel, and the lady who has guided us here indicates clearly that we should literally stand forth and deliver from the altar. "Jesus," I mutter. Even calling it a "podium" or "lectern"—which nobody bothers to do anyway—won't help much now. There's no damned way I'm doing this. It's an altar, complete with all that . . . altar stuff. I'm standing in front of a sash that reads "Behold the Lamb of God," and while this might make for an inspiring tour publicity photo, I'm clearly out of my league here. This is like saluting at The General's tomb, but with much higher stakes. However, there appears no alternative and so, in the evangelical tradition of my fellow Virginians Jerry Falwell and Pat Robertson, I ascend the three small steps to the altar, where I prepare to offer my ennobling message to the not so numerous congregation.

So here we are, at the altar, in the chapel of the old folks home, on the edge of nothing, back in the woods on the far reaches of Hoochville, Nowhere County, in the pouring rain. The audience, now fully assembled, consists of our local contact (a disturbingly cheerful woman with a voice that could worm a sheep), the local Presbyterian preacher (he looks like a bait fisherman), the preacher's wife and her towering hair (you can't swing a dead cat by the tail without hitting hair like that in this part of the Old Dominion). That's the front row. Behind them are four or five residents of the facility, all women, the youngest at least eighty years old. Through my bloodshot eyes I see only a tangled blur of canes and walkers and oxygen tubes. Worst of all, every last one of them is beaming at us in an oddly disconcerting way, as if we have brought the news of their salvation—or perhaps they have only cranked up their oxygen in preparation for our show. My last thought before I begin reading from the altar is that a merciful God would set a twister down exactly here and now. Or . . . *now!* Now? We're beat and so we're just going with a default program of readings without trying to tailor our selections to this surprising "alternative venue." Dan starts off with a reading from Thomas Anburey, a lieutenant in the British Army who was captured in 1777 at the battle of Saratoga. Unaccustomed to the wonders of nature in America, Anburey remarked upon such Virginia marvels as the firefly and the tulip tree, the persimmon and dogwood. In the passage Dan reads, he also describes the wonderful *Didelphis virginiana:*

> . . . we found an opossum, suspended at the extremity of the branch by its tail, which this creature always does when pursued; we sent a servant up the tree, who shook him off, and he fell among the dogs, from whom he did not make the least attempt to escape, but appeared as if dead. It was taken and carried home, all which time it shewed no other signs of life than gently breathing; it was put in a court-yard, where it could not escape, and we watched it for near half an hour, during which it never moved, but lay as dead; at last, it gently raised its head, looking all around, and not perceiving any danger, immediately ran off . . .

So far so good. The old folks are digging the cute possum, and Dan—who really is a charismatic reader—is on a roll. But I'm worried that he may not remember where this particular passage is headed, and he hasn't noticed me trying desperately to catch his eye. Say now, look up, buddy. Look up, Dan. Please look up! He doesn't look up, but instead reads on, enthusiastically:

> . . . we went out and set the dogs at it, and notwithstanding two spirited spaniels worried and shook, nay, even snapped its very bones, which we could distinctly hear, the creature

never shewed any symptoms of life. After the dogs had worried it, and broke almost every bone in its body, which, perhaps you will say, did not reflect much credit to our humanity, a heavy stone was dropt on its head, to end its tortures . . .

Dan finishes this passage, and the room is now so quiet that you could have heard a bone snap—and, given the venue, might have. He is slow to look up from his book, and I am sitting perfectly still, smiling weakly and sweating. For their part, the audience is staring at us blankly. The old folks seem to be gripping their canes more tightly now, perhaps thinking of how satisfying it would be to plunge their rubber tips into our eye sockets.

So the Anburey was a bad call, but we muddle along and after a slo-mo eternity come at last to the final reading—a good concluding selection because it is from Annie Dillard's *Pilgrim at Tinker Creek*, the most famous literary work to celebrate the natural environment of this region. Man, we've got *Pilgrim* here, I think—Pulitzer Prize stuff. We're home free now. I take a deep breath and begin. I can hear the words coming from my mouth—feel them tumbling out into the air in muffled strings—but I'm exhausted and, worse, distracted by the preacher's wife's hair. You just don't see hair like that very often anymore, and its implausible, gravity-defying verticality makes me proud to be a Virginian. I sigh once and begin reading from one of the book's most famous passages:

> I learned to recognize, slowing down, the difference in texture of the light reflected from mudbank, water, grass, or frog. Frogs were flying all around me. At the end of the island I noticed a small green frog. He was exactly half in and half out of the water, looking like a schematic diagram of an amphibian . . .

I look up, hopefully. That's more like it. The audience is coming around now, I can feel it. Never too late for salvation. *Pilgrim* is money in the literary bank, and from the altar I mutter a little prayer of thanks for Dillard's keen eye and graceful prose: *Thanks be to Cousin Annie for this corner pocket shot, which I so desperately need.* More confident now, I continue reading the passage:

> He was a very small frog with wide, dull eyes. And just as I looked at him, he slowly crumpled and began to sag. The spirit vanished from his eyes as if snuffed. His skin emptied and drooped; his very skull seemed to collapse and settle like a kicked tent.

Damn. That's kind of rough with these old people here. And coming from the altar and all. This isn't the uplifting nature story they were expecting—the one with the fluttering butterflies and hopping birds and scarlet-tinted sugar maples that I had seen in paintings on the walls of Shady Meadows as we entered. Besides, this isn't how I remembered the passage. In my mind it was engaging, lyrical natural history, not a snuff film with Kermit in the lead role.

Well, push on. The skull has already collapsed, so it can't get any worse.

> I watched the taut, glistening skin on his shoulders ruck, and rumple, and fall. Soon, part of his skin, formless as a pricked balloon, lay in floating folds like bright scum on top of the water; it was a monstrous and terrifying thing. I gaped bewildered, appalled. An oval shadow hung in the water behind the drained frog; then the shadow glided away. The frog skin bag started to sink.

I look up again, furtively this time. Definitely not good. My geriatric audience is now gaping, bewildered, appalled. These old people are clearly displeased with me, and Dan's possum squishing warm-up act hasn't endeared him to them either. I'm both fried and nervous now, and I can feel a numbing clamminess crawl up my legs even as my scalp feels like it is being dipped in lava. I can't recall where the passage goes from here, but I know I can't possibly end on this note. I vaguely recall that some sort of scientific explanation follows, so I rush ahead:

> "Giant Water Bug" really is the name of the creature, which is an enormous, heavy-bodied brown beetle. It eats insects, tadpoles, fish, and frogs. Its grasping forelegs are mighty and hooked inward. It seizes a victim with these legs, hugs it tight, and paralyzes it with enzymes injected during a vicious bite. That one bite is the only bite it ever takes. Through the puncture shoot the poisons that dissolve the victim's muscles and bones and organs—all but the skin—and through it the giant water bug sucks out the victim's body, reduced to a juice.

Where the hell is that tornado? I sneak a glance at my watch, as if providential relief was annoyingly late to its appointment with my misery. This is now so very bad that I momentarily conclude that perhaps it is not actually happening. I sneak a glance at Dan for a reality check. His face is awkwardly frozen with both jaw and smile set, even as I can distinctly feel him boring a hole in his idiot friend's head with the auger of his mind. The monumental hair now seems to wilt a little, allowing a better view of row two, where several old ladies literally have their mouths open, aghast. I wince a little as I feel the hooch and Whiz begin to roil in my gut. In desperation I skip a couple of the deadlier-looking sentences in the passage I've marked, and go for a quick finish with a few lines that I'm hoping will offer a rational explanation for all this inexorable violence:

> Of course, many carnivorous animals devour their prey alive. The usual method seems to be to subdue the victim by downing or grasping it so it can't flee, then eating it whole or in a series of bloody bites. Frogs eat everything

whole, stuffing prey into their mouths with their thumbs. People have seen frogs with their wide jaws so full of live dragonflies they couldn't close them. Ants don't even have to catch their prey: in the spring they swarm over newly hatched, featherless birds in the nest and eat them tiny bite by bite. That it's rough out there and chancy is no surprise. Every live thing is a survivor on a kind of extended emergency bivouac.

The preacher and the wife and hair are breathless. The fatally cheerful lady is no longer smiling. The old folks are motionless, shocked, devastated.

And now, to my surprise, I feel wash over me a kind of desperate calmness as I realize that recovery is no longer possible. It is too late for salvation, and I am experiencing the woozy, vertiginous feeling of freedom that arrives when there is nothing left to lose. I am filled with the perfect calmness of a condemned man who has asked for a final bowl of buttery grits and a glass of neat whiskey before his execution and has found his last meal perfectly satisfying. After all, what can I do? The mortality cat is out of the nature bag, and nobody can go back to smiling at cute possums or singing frogs again. From my accidental altar I have been preaching the gospel of the food chain to people whose main goal is to avoid becoming part of it. I feel genuinely, tremendously sorry, but my exhaustion has rendered this unimaginable experience profoundly surreal. I wonder if I should ask the God of frogs and men for forgiveness, but I sense it is already too late for that. Little by little, bite by bloody bite, my sermon here has made us all think about floods and tornadoes and pneumonia, about frogs and dragonflies and cancer, ants and flies and oxygen tubes—about stuffing life down our throats with our bony thumbs, or maybe about an angry God stuffing us all, quivering, down the ravenous, gaping maw of nature.

After the reading we gather around the punchbowl because, as Virginians, we must. This civility is our small stay against chaos, our shoring of fragments against the ruin. We try feebly to chat, but even the preacher is too stunned to offer consolation or absolution. There is simply nothing left to say. We now have in common only that we have had our certainties shaken, and yet I clutch at a glimmer of hope that this may still be a great deal to have in common. I deeply regret what has happened, but I also sense that what has been released here is beyond my control. Is the dragonfly immoral for gorging on butterflies, or the frog evil for gorging on dragonflies, or the Giant Water Bug reprehensible for gorging on the frog? In their aquatic phase dragonflies eat tadpoles, so maybe the frog's vicious hunger is the final act of a complex ecological revenge tragedy. And with respect to the Water Bug's fatal embrace, aren't we all scheduled for eventual liquidation? There are no sinners in nature. This is what it is to live in this world, and the force of art is born of its power to reveal the repressed facts of life that we hold before us, invisible, each day. Behold the Lamb of God, surrounded by razor-toothed hunger. At the punchbowl nobody mentions gaping amphibian jaws stuffed full of writhing insects, but I am struck by the strange sense that we have been brought together by some honest fear that lives at the bottom of all our lives. Behind our eyes I see that we are all, young and old together, staring down the dark, insatiable gullet of the world.

It isn't too far to the next Econo-Lodge, and Dan and I are perfectly silent on the drive. By the time we arrive and climb out of the car the rain has given way to a dead, muggy calm. At first I hear nothing but sporadic traffic noise in the distance, but then I am able to isolate a different strain chirping among the humming chorus of cars: frogs. It is frogs, exactly half in and half out of the puddles that have gathered in the low spots of the muddy gravel parking lot behind the hotel.

I wait outside, listening closely and breathing

slowly, while Dan goes to check us in. My experience this week has been deeply humbling, but it has also made clear just how little I ever really cared about a rebel assault on the literary establishment. I needed a six-year excuse to read and write and think about my home, and I don't plan to ask for my money back now. If this week has been unpredictable, comical, disorienting, maybe that is as it should be. We've met some fellow travelers along our way, and we've seen our beautiful home country again. This has been a fine excuse to be in Virginia, and I feel fairly sure that any pilgrimage home is sanctified—even if you're forced to call it a book tour.

I am still numb as we ascend the open, cement stairs to our room, exhausted and silent. I spray Cheez Whiz and pour whiskey and wonder what the General would have done in that Shady Meadows fix—he would have handled that whole thing better, I guess. I click on the tube and we join in progress a black-and-white B movie in which a giant, fast-evolving reptilian beast must harvest and ingest a substantial number of human hypothalamuses (or is it hypothalami?) in order to survive its extended emergency bivouac in this world. The last of the beast's many victims is a professor, whose juicy hypothalamus is apparently considered especially savory. *Bon appetit.* I turn off the TV, roll over, and think about book tours, about my new old friends at Shady Meadows, about art and nature and mortality. My last waking thought is how good it feels to be back home in Virginia. The puddle-dwelling frogs sing me to sleep, and in my sleep I dream of dragonflies.

Kelly Cherry

Why the Figure of Christ Keeps Turning Up in My Work

My sister thinks I shouldn't let anyone know what our childhood was like. "It was not a normal childhood," she says. "It's better not to talk about it. It's better not to *think* about it." She says she is ashamed of our childhood and that she feels other people would look at us strangely if they knew about it.

Nevertheless, we were not mistreated the way, one notes sorrowfully, so many children are. No, it was simply that, for long periods of time—for years on end—our parents were distracted, and forgot that we were around.

My sister has a clearer memory for these years than I do; I was a dreamy kid, as distracted by my own thoughts as my parents were by theirs. "'Don't you remember," my sister asks me, "that we were not even taught to brush our teeth until we went to school? The school nurse was shocked."

I reply that our parents undoubtedly thought there was no point in worrying about baby teeth that were destined to fall out.

"For one cold winter in the country," she goes on, referring to the year after we had moved away from the tenement flat in upstate New York, "I had no mittens because nobody noticed that I needed a pair."

I do remember that winter. The furnace didn't run, and my sister and I were not allowed to turn on the kerosene heater. After school, she and I would huddle together under our coats in the scratchy upholstered armchair, listening to "Sergeant Preston of the Yukon" and other radio shows until our parents got home from work.

We were kids on the loose, kids at large. The neighbors told my parents that I was a "child of nature," and my parents thought this was a scream and teasingly repeated the epithet to me, never realizing that what the neighbors meant by it was that my hair needed combing.

What had consumed their attention so, leaving them little to give to their children's socialization, was music. They were string quartet violinists. But this is not to say that our family lived a life of intellectual glamour and elegance. Despite people's notions of string quartets and string quartet playing, it is possible to be a string quartet player in the same way that a poet is likely to be a poet: poor and taking on other kinds of work to make the poetry possible. My parents were poor and took on other kinds of work to make their string quartet playing possible. Not until their later years did my parents enter the ranks of the economically middle class, and even then they were always afraid some financial disaster would, without warning, catapult them back out of it.

There were *moments* of glamour and elegance, though, and more important, there were whole days and nights of the most astonishing beauty imaginable—right there in the living room, where my parents and the violist and the cellist were making the room blue with smoke. There was an ashtray on every footstool and a footstool beside every player. There was a cup of cocoa on my mother's footstool and a cup of coffee on everybody else's footstool. Nobody ever used a footstool as a footstool. My parents' music stands were black iron, heavy as armament; the violist's and cellist's music stands would be the aluminum ones that you can fold up and carry to rehearsal. My parents had these music stands too, for when they went elsewhere to play. When they went elsewhere, my sister and I were again kids on the loose, kids at large. (We were also kids with the music of Beethoven in our hearts and on our minds.)

They worked so hard, our parents did, what with trying to earn enough money to get by and then practicing and rehearsing and performing on top of that, that even if they had wanted to—and really, they didn't want to—they had no time or energy to think about us. And if they couldn't be bothered to teach us how to comb our hair or brush our teeth, they certainly couldn't be bothered to teach us religion. We never went to church. Who had time to go to church? Moreover, who would *want* to go to church and have to say hello to people? My parents didn't much like people. People were dumb bosses, busybody neighbors, and other undesirable two-legged creatures.

As for God, my mother, at least, had her doubts. She felt that the only goodness in the historical world had been accomplished by a handful of exceptional beings, most of them composers or artists or scientists (writers had a perverse predilection for focusing on the ugliness of the world). So far as she could see, if there was a God, he wasn't a very smart one. Or he was cruel, causing suffering in a way that at least looked malicious and, if it wasn't that, was at best callous. She felt some guilt about harboring these doubts—she knew that her mother and father in Mississippi would have been distressed by them and, even more discomfitingly, might feel sorry for her for having to endure them—but she was a tough-minded thinker with a deep distaste for people's ability to fool themselves. People *were* foolish. People would settle for anything, even Bruckner.

The one time we visited our grandparents in Gulfport, Mississippi, my sister and I were spirited off to the Presbyterian church, where we were given a copy of the Shorter Catechism and told to memorize it. *What is a man's chief end? Man's chief end is to glorify God, and to glorify Him forever.* I remember the cool stone walls of the church, lilies and irises heaped at the altar, the satiny polished wood of the pews, fans like Ping-Pong paddles, and hymnals with their lovely thin pages waiting in the pockets of the backrests.

What is man's chief end? It is to glorify God and to enjoy Him forever.

I thought these words were wonderful—although to be honest, I was even more impressed with my ability to recite the Catechism. (There were 107 questions and answers.) Perhaps it was the first time that my demonstrated ability to do something, as differentiated from my potential to fulfill parental fantasies of success, had been important to anyone. Perhaps I just liked the process of learning, the way I had liked learning how to spell *sulfanilamide*, saying the syllables over and over, pleased as punch by their phonetic charm.

We had moved back down South before I had another encounter with religion. It was the year I turned ten. For my birthday, my grandmother, who clearly thought that the Shorter Catechism was but a beginning, sent me a Bible. It was the King James Version, it had a black, grained cover and a zipper, and because it was the first book I had ever owned by myself, I thought I should read it. And so I did, working my way through the begats to Job, and on to the major and minor prophets and onward still to the New Testament, not skipping a word because skipping would be cheating, right up to Mark 16:16, which so offended me that I drew a blue-ink box around the verse and stared and stared at it: "He that believeth and is baptized shall be saved; but he that believeth not shall be damned." I still have this Bible—which, however, my dog ate a good part of a few years ago, becoming thereby, I should think, an unusually holy dog, eucharistic in the extreme—and when l open it to Mark I find that blue-ink square, drawn in a ten-year-old hand.

Enraged, I carried the Bible downstairs. My parents were sitting in the kitchen. "Read this," I commanded, and they obeyed.

"Well?" they asked, lifting their eyebrows. (My father was handsome, and my mother was beautiful, and my father could lift one eyebrow at a time.)

"It's a bribe!" I said. "I don't think this is right! If you're good you go to heaven, and if you're bad you go to hell. But you ought to want to be good without being promised a heaven, and you ought to want not to be bad without being threatened with a hell."

As I remember it, that is very close to what I actually said.

I am sure that my parents thought this, too, was a scream.

At the same time, they were the kind of people who worry about such things, and so a debate ensued on whether heaven and hell were bribe and threat or merely the consequences of one's behavior, assuming that heaven and hell existed, which they probably didn't, because if they did they weren't working very well to keep things in order on earth and if they existed there would have to be a God but if there were a God you'd think He could come up with a better idea, one that would work. I finished reading the Bible—it would have been cheating not to—but I was skeptical. I had written a story titled "Tiny Angelcake," about an angel named Angelcake (whom everyone called Pieface). Pieface wanted to take a present to the baby Jesus lying in a manger in Bethlehem but was short on funds. On the way there he met The Three Wise Men. "What," said The Three Wise Men, "are you doing here?"

"Going to see the Messiah," answered the angel.

"Keeping up with the news! Ha, ha, ha!" They laughed and went on their way.

When Pieface got to the manger where Jesus lay, he found he still had nothing to give Him, so he composed a poem, of which I remember that two lines went something like this:

For thou art the Son of God
Even though many things He does to us seem
very odd.

But we were living in the Bible Belt now, and the next year we moved closer to town. There was a man in the house next to ours who said everything wrong—the rose bushes, he complained, were being attacked by *asps*—and across the back way there lived a divorcee in a large ramshackle house with a mulberry tree in the side yard. At one end of the block that our house was on there was a combination lunchroom and beer joint. And at the other end of the block there was a woman who invited the neighborhood children to come to her house after school to hear stories from the New Testament. I had been rejected by the Brownies—"We think your daughter will be happier in some other organization," the women who led the troop told my mother—and I was relieved to find that the invitation included me. We sat on the floor. She had cutouts of the Bible characters that she moved around on a green felt board. Somehow the colorful figures adhered to the board. The figures' robes were bright, and some of the figures carried staffs or jugs of wine and water, and there were houses and sheep, and children too, all living in a place that was always sunny. When I had a chance to go to Bible summer school I quickly agreed, riding the bus every day into the city. There, at the church, I learned to make a beanie.

When our neighborhood church started its own Vacation Bible School, I was, therefore, ready. I had never been to church in this church, but I knew what to expect from Vacation Bible School. This time I learned to make a purse. It was white, and it had a rope handle that you pulled on to make the purse open and shut. But this Bible school didn't last for long, because the preacher, whose wife taught the purse-making class, had knocked up the neighborhood divorcee.

As a fiscally if not morally responsible preacher, he had saved some money to support the divorcee during her confinement, but instead she left town to have her baby. In her absence, to redeem his reputation, the preacher held a week-long revival in a large tent near the mulberry tree.

Figuring he'd better not harp on the evils of sex, he opted for the evils of alcohol. Night after night he harangued the penitent. As for the unrepentant, "This very night," he shouted, "God in His wrath may strike dead some sinner who, instead of being here at this revival, is sitting on a barstool in a beer joint!"

While the preacher was uttering these words, a young man sitting on a barstool in the beer joint at the end of the block that our house was on keeled over with a heart attack. The next night the preacher had two new converts—Ike and Ida, the proprietors of the tavern.

"We want to dedicate our lives to Christ," Ida declared.

"We'd stop selling beer right now," Ike, who wore an *I Like Ike* button, explained, "and just run a lunchroom, but we don't know what to do with the twenty cases of beer we have stored in the pantry."

The preacher promised to give the matter careful consideration. The next morning, he'd come up with a solution. He drove to the tavern, bought all the beer that was stored in the pantry, and loaded it in the back of his old station wagon. That night, at the revival meeting, he told the congregation how Ike and Ida had been born again and how he had used his savings to buy all the beer in the pantry to free them from temptation. "Saturday afternoon," he announced, "there will be a picnic near the bridge at Rattlesnake Creek. You are all invited. There will be sandwiches and soft drinks, and the beer'll be poured into the creek." And then he added, "Hallelujah!"

Well, everyone was so impressed that the collection plate overflowed, and for days thereafter contributions came in via the mail. There was enough money for a new station wagon, which Mrs. Preacher drove when she did her grocery shopping.

Ike and Ida stayed saved, but before long there was another beer joint at the other end of Jahnke Road, just a little farther down from the house where I used to go to hear Bible stories. And what, oh what, I wonder now, became of the divorcee and her love child?

Even though my family didn't go to church, or attend revivals, living in the Bible Belt I heard a good deal of talk about God. Finally, when I was twelve, I went to my mother. "What do you think about all this?" I asked. "Do you believe in God?"

She answered me by putting a record on the turntable. It was a late Beethoven quartet. "I don't know whether or not there's a God," she said, "but I know there was a Beethoven, and that's good enough for me."

It set high standards, this love of Beethoven did—and the love of Bach—and yet I would not for anything trade the years of being enthralled by this music and of trying to fathom it: of trying to understand what it was saying and of trying to figure out how to say, in words, what it was saying. I wrote a long "Letter to Myself" in which I vowed that I would never forget what it *really* meant to be an artist, any artist. What it really meant, I believed, was to listen to the deepest soundings of the heart and the most elevated commandments of the soul and encode these discoveries in the eternal, communicative forms of art. I don't suppose I had any idea of how this might be done, but I believed it was what one had to do. To tell the truth, I even believed it was what one had been born to do.

In those days, however, even if you had been born to do it, you could not do it in college. If you were female, the presumption was that you would not do it even after college until, say, you were well married or established in a "real" profession and had time on the side to mess around with something a little more fanciful, except that by then you'd have outgrown those romantic notions. If my parents knew enough to know that even girls, even Southern girls, could be deeply serious about their artistic ambitions, they were that much more bitter about the hard life that went with such ambitions and that much more determined to steer their elder daughter in a different direction. I shortly found myself, for example, studying math and science, often in unexpected places like the New Mexico Institute of Mining and Technology.

In the absence of writing classes—for there were none at the schools I attended—I had dreamed of permission to major in philosophy. I had dreamed of this permission from the age of fourteen, and I got it in my last year, after six transfers to five schools, two of which I'd been kicked out of; and I got it after a six-month respite dictated by the fact that we could find no college anywhere that would have me, during which period my mother kept telling me I now had two choices in life: my math credits qualified me to be a Grade 4 civil servant. Or I could go to a place in Florida where I would be trained to run a motel. (The magazines, at this time, were full of ads for these schools where you could learn how to run a motel. Our nation had fallen in love with the idea of taking vacations, with the idea of being able to *drive* to vacation, with the idea of a vacation *being* driving.)

During that six-month enforced stay out of school, I read, in *TIME* magazine, which was the closest I'd ever gotten to a literary periodical, about a French girl named Francoise Sagan, who had published a novel. This was the first clue I had that books could be written by live female people. I had previously thought that becoming a writer worked like this: first, you studied a subject that would help you to get a job. Next, you got the job, and, while taking care of a husband and children, and working, you wrote a book. Eventually you grew old, and no doubt tired, too, and you died, and then the book was published. Probably, along the way, somewhere in between your writing the book and its getting published posthumously, you also suffered a sex change and became male.

I was the same age as Sagan—eighteen—so I followed her example and wrote a novella, encouraged by visions of reviews in *TIME*. But I didn't understand that what made her book newsworthy was not just her age but her subject matter, sex. I didn't know very much about sex and what I did know about it didn't seem very literary to me. Instead, for one hundred pages, I narrated the rediscovery of the Ten Commandments after the nuclear holocaust of World War III. The protagonist vaguely resembled Moses. There was a dead silver crow that functioned as a crucifixion image—the title was *The Silver Crow*. I guess I thought I knew a little something about religion, though looking back, I am not sure that I did not know more about sex.

This novella failed to make me famous but it did convince my parents to give up on the science idea and let me major in philosophy. I loved the rigor of philosophy, the hardcore up-against-the-wall cut-the-crap kind of philosophy that looked on philosophy of religion or political philosophy or aesthetics with disdain. But I also, secretly, loved philosophy of religion and political philosophy and aesthetics. I read Aquinas and Augustine and briefly consulted with a Dominican priest, but I couldn't consent to the hierarchical structure of Catholicism, its sacerdotal bias—all those men with catechistic answers to questions I preferred to ask for myself—and, too, my aesthetic propensities were for white-frame churches or churches with cool stone walls bare of ornament. Also, I didn't believe in God.

By the time I left graduate school, I realized why my parents had been so eager for me to become a scientist. All my work in philosophy qualified me for a job at sixty dollars a week as an editorial assistant for the Presbyterian Board of Christian Education in Richmond. I was still paying rent on the empty apartment in Charlottesville because the landlady wouldn't let me out of my lease, and my parents were good Calvinists who wouldn't have dreamed of letting me just not pay.

Despite the low pay—young men with my qualifications were earning five times as much—this was a great job. I got to spend all day reading the Bible and the dictionary. I worked at the Board from eight in the morning till four-thirty in the afternoon. At four-thirty, I went to my nighttime job, where until eleven I typed addresses on envelopes (later, I was promoted to the position of writing fake histories for overseas orphans whose real histories were unknown, so that their stateside sponsors would feel closer to them). On weekends I freelanced, writing the script for a biblical filmstrip, or revising church literature so that it could be recorded for the blind. I wrote my poems and stories during lunch hour, in the ladies' room. Working this way, I managed to save enough money to go to Europe, and when I came back from Europe, I entered a graduate program in creative writing—I had not known before that there were any such programs—and was for the first time wholly happy in school, and then, because at twenty-five I was an old maid, but also because he was marvelously intellectually exciting, and a thrilling person to talk with, I married a sculptor who had come down from New York City to teach for one semester. He was Jewish, and his family disowned him for marrying me. The wedding took place over the Christmas holidays, and there was a Christmas tree in the living room, but we made sure to omit any reference to Christ in the service, and we put a Moslem ornament on the top of the tree-but his parents still refused to be present, and they wrote him out of the will.

My in-laws might have liked for me to convert, but I was much too stubborn to do something like that just to please people I hadn't even met—they declined to meet me—and, of course, as I now see, if I had converted I would have obviated the point my husband was making by marrying me. No, I didn't consider conversion until *afterward*—after the marriage had ended, after the divorce. We had been living in New York, and after our divorce, I stayed on there, taking on a variety of jobs. One of them was writing an analytic teacher's guide to a collection of Jewish morality tales for a Judaica publishing house. I had protested to the publisher that I knew nothing about Jewish morality tales, but he was unfazed. He sat me down at a small typing table two feet away from his own desk, so there was no way I could not do the work that had been set before me, which was to think about certain stories from the Torah and the Midrash and the Talmud and so forth and try to understand them. And plainly, this was another wonderful job. It would have been grand to have had the access to early publication that writers have now, to have had celebrity teachers who could hand me over to their agents or refer me to writers' colonies, to have had time off with the aid of literary grants, and I would never undervalue the sense of professionalism and, often, the self-confidence that the structure of today's literary world promotes, but if I had had those things I would have missed out not only on the amazing teachers I did have but also on several years of deep involvement with theological tradition. I might never have learned how to sit still at a typing table and *think*—and my boss *always* knew when I wasn't *thinking*. He seemed not in the least to mind that my interpretation of these Jewish morality tales was markedly Calvinist. There is a generation of children who went to synagogues on Long Island and grew up on my Calvinist interpretations of Jewish morality tales.

One weekend something happened to me that upset me greatly. I called my boss and said that 1 would not be able to come in to work because I planned to kill myself. (And I meant it.) "Let's have lunch first," he said, "at Max's Kansas City."

Seated in the booth, I told him what had happened. "What a wonderful story that would make," he said. "Write it."

"Oh no, I'll never ever write anything again," I said. I had not written anything in a long time, having concluded from certain life experiences, not to mention my husband's restrictive opinions of women in general, that a woman's wanting to write, or at least my wanting to write, *was* a romantic notion. I was completely without any kind of confidence in myself, whether about writing or anything else, and every morning the first thing I did upon waking was remind myself that I was *not* a writer and must not presume to be one.

"Then don't write a story," he said. "Write me a letter. Just put in it exactly what you've told me today."

So I wrote my boss, whom I hardly knew, a letter. And rewrote it and rewrote it. I wrote it over a dozen times, and then I gave it to him. It was still only about sixteen pages long. "This is interesting," he said. "'I'm going to show it to my friend the writer."

He had a friend who was a writer, and he let this friend use one of the company desks and a typewriter and telephone every day. He carried my letter to his friend, who, a half-hour later, came into our room and said, "You need a scene here and here and here." And he made little X's in the right-hand margin everywhere he thought I needed a scene.

I worked on the story for the next six months, and when it was done, at something over forty pages, I took it in to the office. The friend said, "Now send this to—" and he named a prestigious magazine published by a Jewish organization. I had not sent my work out before, though a few things had found their way into publication, and I sent the story where he told me to send it. It came back by return mail. The editor had attached a note. "If you want to know why I rejected this," the note said, "call my secretary."

"Call his secretary," the friend said.

"I can't!"

"You can use the telephone in here," my boss said.

So I called the editor's secretary, and in a few hours a messenger arrived with a slip of paper on which several questions had been noted in pencil. As I remember, they were rather broad: "What does the title mean? Why does the story end the way it does?"

I was sure that what I was supposed to do now was give up. "No, no, no," the friend said. "What you are supposed to do now is wait three weeks, reread the story, make the changes that it will then be apparent to you are needed, and send the story back."

"Send it back? After it's been rejected? Won't he think I'm pestering him?"

But I did what the friend said, and three weeks later I discovered that the editor's questions, though broad, had been precisely to the point. This time I heard not by return mail, not by messenger—the phone rang, and it was the editor, and he was accepting my story, which made use of the idea of covenant and commented on many odd things that seemed to have been done to humankind.

"The only thing is," he said, "'there are too many obscenities in it. You'll have to cut some."

Well, I went to work cutting obscenities. I cut every obscenity I thought I could cut and sent the story back to the editor. He telephoned a second time. "You've cut too many obscenities," he said. "We'll have to put some back."

By this time, my boss was making me use the telephone in the showroom. We had an ecumenical showroom, and there were nuns browsing among the books, and a rabbi or two eating lunch from paper bags at the long table. The editor, at his end of the line, and I, at my end of the line, proceeded to have a thoroughly filthy conversation discussing which of the original dirty words should be restored. And when the story came out, with all these dirty words, I went to the dry cleaner's to pick up my dry cleaning, and the tailor looked at the name on his slip and said, "I just read your story! Let me call my wife!" And he called, "Queenie, come here!" and his wife appeared from behind a curtain, and they both shook my hand, and I signed the receipt for him as an autograph, and he handed over my dry cleaning and I walked home so full of confidence I was ready to burst with it. I had confidence to spare, confidence to give to all and sundry.

I had begun attending a conversion class. I was the only member of the class who was neither en-gaged nor recently married to a Jew, but as I say, it was only after I'd been divorced from a Jew that I felt I could legitimately consider converting to Judaism. There was much in the tradition that attracted me, and I completed the class with every expecta-tion of going through the conversion ceremony. And then something happened: I realized I could *not* go through with it. I realized that what had been pro-pelling me along this particular course was a politi-cal sympathy, a sense that in an unjust world the only just act is to align oneself with the victims of injustice. If we were not part of the solution, we were part of the problem.

But when class was over, and I held my certificate in my hand and it was time to convert, I found, welling up in me, a hitherto unrecognized attachment to, of all unexpected things, the figure of *Christ*. I could not let go of this figure that had, all unknown to me, become a part of my deepest self. In fact, it was the figure of Christ that, to me, explained my attraction to Judaism. Here was the emotional heart of my passion for justice.

I still didn't believe in God. God, you see, was never what any of this was about. . . .

I put the certificate, which I still treasure, in a footlocker with other treasures (mostly early manuscripts, some photographs and letters, a valentine from my husband, when he had been my husband), and started trying to figure out what this *was* about. In a long poem titled "A Bird's-Eye View of Einstein," I tried to grasp the idea of the Trinity—the mathematical mystery of three-in-one—by stealing a tack from the theory of relativity. I built the poem in three parts, naturally, interpreting the Son or Bridegroom through my ex-husband, the Holy Ghost through my brother, and God the father through my father; where relativity comes in is that I let my point of view slide in a rather peculiar way through all three parts, bending the time of the poem back on itself. Though the plan of triads is carried out extensively— there are mini-sermons alluding to the three major prophets of the Old Testament (Jeremiah, Ezekiel, Isaiah), dramatizations of the breaking of the three Freudian taboos (cannibalism, incest, murder), and so on through strata of trinities—it was the linking of them through point of view that was what the poem was about. And that linkage culminated in an image of the crucifixion—rather, to be frank, a brutal image, in which the narrator's murderous complicity is made clear, as well as the narrator's self-abnegation in favor of the very thing she has destroyed.

It was a perilously difficult poem to write, demanding as much concentration as I was capable of and so painful that I frequently wept and then had to write on spiral notebook pages that were wet and that smeared the ink. I wrote it while I was teaching at a university in southwest Minnesota, during the break between quarters. I wrote it at night, through the night, emerging into the morning light blinded and monomaniacal. With the students gone, with snow on the ground for as far as the eye could see—and the eye could see very far in that flat, beautiful but desolate landscape—I was cut loose from the world, as if I had been cast into outer space. I would shut the door to my office, and it was like going into a space capsule that would carry me to constellations of thought and feeling that had previously seemed unreachable or whose existence I had not even suspected. Night after night I read The Gospel According to St. John and The Book of Revelation, and it was a revelation to me how inextricably bound I was to this figure of the abandoned Christ and how much responsibility I felt I bore for things gone wrong, love ungranted. For love unfulfilled in action, and for wrongdoing that inhibits right doing. I learned, with the force of pure feeling, just what crimes I was capable of, and it was out of this struggle with myself that I made this poem about the crucified Christ. In the end, it was, perhaps, less a conventionally Christian poem than a poem of eternal recurrence, a stoic acknowledgment of the eternal cycle of despair and hope, sin and redemption, grief and triumph.

In an autobiographical narrative, *The Exiled Heart*, in which I try to know what I can about the nature of freedom and the meaning of love—a task I had set myself because I was engaged to a Latvian composer I had met in Moscow on that first trip to Europe—but Brezhnev's KGB prevented our marriage—I found myself turning again to the figure of Christ, crucified and risen, as a way to think about these subjects. Even now it would be difficult for me to say that I believe in God, even the most sophisticatedly defined kind of God. I was raised to be a doubter, and I'll go on doubting until I can put my hands through holes. But here is the thing: the issue of belief, for me, I now see, is a *secondary* one. I have finally figured out that belief is the question that arises in the *middle* of the discourse, and the discourse itself is Christ. I have figured out that the language I think with, the language I have thought with since I first began to think, is the figure of Christ. "In the beginning was the Word, and the Word was with God, and the Word was God." It is through the figure of Christ that I have come the closest to saying what I want to say—what I believe I have heard music saying to me. This is not to say that I think or write only about the figure of Christ. Obviously not. But the figure of Christ is central to everything I write, whether it is there on the page or not. It is the "word" I write with, even when it is not the word I write. In the Logos we have been given a language that can speak the silences, that can say what we may not dare say otherwise, a language that allows us to think about every aspect of the world, human and inhuman, about even those aspects that might otherwise frighten us into the silence of children without parents, which is what we all, ultimately, are—left alone, forgotten. I would not for one minute say it is the only language, but it is my language, my native language.

Still, as I write these words, I can hear someone objecting to the—what do we say?—the maleness of this language. I hear that feminist chorus that would rather say goddess than god, that finds a male Christ insufficiently androgynous. I am sympathetic to the sense of disenfranchisement that these voices seek to correct, but for myself, it is exactly that maleness that I am unwilling to give up: I want a language that lets me think beyond myself. I want a language through whose agency I am able to transcend my own hungry ego. I want a wider view of the world than I can obtain only through my own eyes. I want to know the Other. I want, that is, to be a writer. In this respect, I sometimes think, I may actually be more fortunate than men writers today. The ground of female being is a territory less literarily charted than the ground of male being. A woman writer, if she has an adventurous spirit, can go anywhere, and almost everywhere she goes will be a new and subtle place, rich in unexplored implications, epiphanous, unexhausted. She can *translate* herself, as it were, to places the reader has never been, or does not yet realize he has been.

She can say what it is like to have been there.

And if she does, she will be dedicated to a purpose that is chief, glorious, and joyful forever. At least, this is what I believe. I believe that we *must* say all that it is within our power to say, and we *must* think about all that it is within our power to think about. Our lives, let us say, are sentences, life sentences, surrounded by a silence so profound that it is tautological, a preface and an epilogue of pure silence. We speak them, and they are uttered against such a silence as is terrifying, and salutary, to contemplate.

Michael Chitwood

The Hunt Fund

When his gun went off, I jumped, bumping against the tree. Then the deer was crashing down the hill toward me. It sounded big as a cow. Just as it got to the creek bank 25 yards in front of me, it disappeared behind a tangle of honeysuckle vines and saplings. I had the gun raised and the safety off. The deer would probably step out in a moment. From the blast of adrenaline my body had given itself, I started to shake.

"When did this get planned?" my wife asked as we dressed for work one morning, a week before season opened.

"Back in the summer," I answered.

My father and brother hunt the entire opening week of deer season in Virginia. They go to the grocery store together to buy supplies and fill the back of Dad's Bronco with food, clothes, a Coleman stove, pots, plastic dishes, and utensils. It's a family joke now that Dad stashes money away all year for the Hunt Fund, and he pays for everything during the week out of the fund.

I explained to my wife that I just wanted to get my share of the Hunt Fund. She pulled a towel from the closet and shut the bathroom door.

In late October and early November, whitetail deer become very active. They show up in odd places. The local paper will probably have a story about a terrified deer rampaging through a shopping mall parking lot or breaking its neck trying to leap a backyard privacy fence in a well-populated subdivision. They aren't frightened by hunters. In most places, deer season doesn't open until the middle of November. The deer are in rut. The males will follow the females wherever they go. The males will also try to run other males away from their tract of woods. It makes for recklessness.

Because deer now have no natural predator other than man, the population, in many parts of the country, has outstripped the available territory. Deer have moved into the suburbs.

Any hunter who says he hunts to keep down the deer population, to maintain nature's balance, is a liar.

I grew up hunting, mostly rabbits. Every Saturday during rabbit season, from the time I was about 12 years old until I was about 17, my father and I would join Franklin Furrow, Dad's friend, and his son Rodney, my good friend, for a day of hunting. Many times other men and boys would come along.

My father and Franklin Furrow both had beagles. Most of the dogs were related. Our best jump dog was the daughter of Franklin's best jump dog. Sally and Dixie would sniff so hard inside a brushpile that they actually snorted. If there was a rabbit in there, he was coming out.

There were rules. You didn't shoot a rabbit on the jump. We wanted to hear the dogs run. You never shot in the direction of a person or dog. If the dogs jumped a deer, you didn't continue hunting until all the dogs came back. Rabbits run in a circle and won't go very far from where they are flushed. A deer will leave the voting district. Sometimes we had to stop the rabbit hunt, get in the truck and go find the dogs. We'd drive along back roads with the windows down. Two men and two boys packed in a truck cab, listening.

My brother was working his way down the hill from his stand, toward the creek. Either his shot had hit the deer, and it had died behind the honeysuckle or it would flush very shortly.

I walked toward the tangle with my rifle up. The deer broke away from us, heading up the creek. Picking them up and putting them down, as my father says.

How can you be so surprised when fully prepared? I swung and fired. I don't know where the first shot hit. I know it wasn't the deer. The second shot hit a pine tree square in the middle. The deer disappeared into the woods.

My brother and I walked to the tangle of honeysuckle the deer had hid behind. The leaves were splattered with bright blood. It was crimson, almost unnaturally red.

"Damn it, damn it, damn it," my brother said, taking off his cap. "I *thought* I hit that deer. Damn it." He walked up the creek a little way then walked back. He looked in the direction the deer had gone as though he might be able to see it. "Damn it," he said. "I hate that."

I work in an office in the Research Triangle Park, North Carolina. My wife works in an office in the Park. About 34,000 people come to work each day in the Park. It's one of the largest concentrations of Ph.D.s and engineers in the United States. We all work in offices or laboratories--8, 10, 12 hours inside each day. When we have finished working, most of us drive home and go inside our houses. Maybe we go to the mall or catch a movie.

More than likely, you're inside right now. When was the last time you were seriously cold? Which direction was the wind blowing today? Was it cloudy when the sun came up this morning? If you stood in your yard would it be quiet enough to hear a leaf striking bare branches on its way to the ground?

The company I work for has just purchased equipment for research in virtual reality. The engineers tell me that eventually you will be able to drive through a town, walk through a house or rearrange the furniture in a room without moving from in front of the computer monitor. You can even have virtual sex, and it's much safer than the real thing.

Our best jump dog was an escape artist. She was a master hunter and hated the confinement of the dog lot. I would watch from my sister's bedroom to discover the latest escape route. Sometimes she found a soft spot and tunneled under the fence. Other times it was over the top, climbing by hooking her forepaws over the wire and pushing with her hind legs.

After she was almost hit on the highway during one of her breakouts, Dad rigged a leash to slide on a wire inside the lot. It gave her run of the place and still kept her safe.

It was my job to feed the dogs each day after school, a chore I did with varying degrees of promptness. Sally's body was stiff when I found it dangling halfway down the outside of the fence. She must have come over sometime that morning. I cradled her cold rigid body to free one hand to unsnap the leash, her noose. Her awkward stiffness and my tears made it a difficult task.

"We'll have to track it," my brother says, still pacing up and down the creek bank. He has been spanking his leg with his cap. Now he puts it back on and starts off in the direction the deer went. He's crouched, scanning the leaves.

"Here," he points to a few splotches of blood. "You stand here," he says. He moves ahead. "OK, here's some more," he says, pointing to where he wants me to stand. I wait while he scouts the forest floor. If he doesn't see anything after twenty yards or so, he comes back to me and heads in a different direction.

Dawn in the woods is slow motion. The light soaks in like a drizzle. The landscape forms out of the darkness like the images on a Polaroid. Christmas morning, and there, materializing, is the happy boy with his new shotgun.

The squirrel was working a pine cone. My father whispered in my ear, so close his Saturday stubble scraped my face.

"Take a deep breath and squeeze the trigger; don't jerk it."

He braced me with his chest at my back, his arms around me in a light hug. All during church the next day, I touched my shoulder, proud of the tenderness.

Our stands are homemade. I had helped my father and brother set them up a week before the season opened. "This is a good place," my brother said as he tightened the chain that held the stand to the tree. "I got that big one here two years ago."

The stand is a ladder with a small platform on top. The platform has a semi-circle cut into it, which fits around the trunk of a tree. You find a tree the correct size and lash the stand to it. It's best to choose a smooth tree because it will be your back rest.

You should get to your stand before daylight. You climb up, keeping your rifle pointed away from you. You turn carefully and sit down. Your feet rest on the topmost rung. Settle in, you're going to be here awhile.

Still-hunting is our native Zen. You must remain as quiet as possible. You must be absolutely alert. You can scan about 200 degrees of the circle of surrounding landscape without straining unduly. You must listen into the other 160 degrees.

I stopped hunting during my college years. I was the first member of my family, my extended family including grandparents, aunts, uncles and cousins, to attend a residential college, which meant I was away during most of hunting season. Also, thanks to some courses I had taken, I had questions about hunting. Mostly, though, it was just because I was away.

My brother did not go to college. His hunting experience is seamless. My education, which my parents paid for, allowed me to get a good job, inside, at a desk far from my home county.

My brother is a heavy equipment operator, by all accounts one of the best in the county. He lives four miles from my parents on land purchased with money my parents gave him, the equivalent of the sum required for my college education. Which is more real, an idea or an acre?

The week before season opened a deer was killed at the mouth of our exit onto Interstate 40. It must have been hit by an eighteen wheeler because it was reduced to fairly small pieces that were scattered along the highway, on the shoulder and in the middle of the road.

All week long, the commuters, speaking into cellular phones, sipping their coffee from wide-bottomed mugs, catching up on the world with National Public Radio, rendered the chunks of meat into a long red stain.

There was a scooped out place in the leaves and a large splash of blood at the center of it. "He lay down for a while," my brother said. We tracked the blood trail for about a mile. "It shouldn't be much farther," my brother said.

Three hundred yards more and we saw the deer standing in the woods. Some of his intestines were dangling in the leaves. My brother dropped to one knee and brought the cross-hairs of his scope to bear. The deer fell with his shot. When we got to the deer we discovered that the first shot had broken his right hind leg.

"I'm glad we found you," my brother said to the deer as he pulled intestines and lungs from the chest cavity. He was field dressing the animal so the meat would be in the best shape possible. He was up to his elbows inside the deer. "I would have felt terrible if we hadn't found you."

When the breeze stirs, the stand sways with the tree. You sway with the stand and the tree. It's a gentle dance because the roots have a solid hold.

My father had a business meeting he couldn't skip on the second morning of deer season, but he came home at noon to see if we had any luck. We had my brother's deer in the back of his pickup.

We told my father the story of the creek and the tracking. My brother and I told it in tandem, each breaking in to add details or mention landmarks we knew our father would know.

"I hate it, but I've got to go back to work," Dad said after we'd finished. He handed me a twenty dollar bill.

"Y'all get some lunch. This week everything's on the Hunt Fund."

We've thrown a chain across the biggest limb of the maple at the side of the house to hold the buck while we skin it.

"You'll have to lift him up until I can get the chain hooked," my brother says. I hook my hands under the buck's front legs in a kind of hug and strain to lift him.

"A little higher."

I have to get a better grip. I pull the deer to me, brace him against my chest. My face is buried in the brown, black and grey of his shoulder. It's all I can do to get him high enough.

Casey Clabough

The Skeleton Woman

"Tell them I am going to show them what they are." This from my mother while dropping me off at primary school.

She'd agreed to come to Parent Show and Tell Day but we had to report to the teacher what our visiting parent would be talking about. I leaned forward to hug her and she kissed me on the forehead. I always looked up at her, reluctant to go.

"Go on now," she'd say after a moment.

But once I was out of the car I'd always turn around and wave, as if the hug and the kiss hadn't been enough. She would smile a warm, slow smile and then shoo me on with a flick of her wrist.

I'd walk away slowly so long as I could feel her eyes on my back. But when I sensed them move and heard the car pull away, I would stop and walk back, watching as she pulled out onto the road in front of the school. Her car was very loud and rumbled like a faraway storm. Unless a teacher made me move, I would wait listening until it reached the place half a mile away where the speed changed from 25 to 55. Then I would hear the sudden burst of sound that came when Mama stomped the floor. She didn't know it, but that was her real daily goodbye to me.

"Go, Mama!" I would say in my mind and wonder if she heard me.

Her car was an old Mercury Cougar she'd bought years ago, before she quit her job. It had an engine called a V8, like the drink I liked.

"Its getting old, like me," she'd say sometimes,

"but its still got plenty of power. More than three hundred horses worth."

"My dad's going to bring his axe," announced a boy to our circle of boys. "He's a pulpwood cutter."

"Cool," said one of the other boys. "Mine works on cars. He's going to tell about an engine he helped build for a race car driver named Ward Burton."

The first one looked at me. "What's your dad gonna show?"

Me. "My dad can't make it, so my mom's coming."

"What does your mom do?"

Me, shrugging. "She stays at home a lot."

First boy. "Ha! That means she's a housewife."

"They don't even have jobs," another boy said. "What could she tell about? They just stay at home and do what dads say."

"Yeah," said the first one. "Think of how dumb that would be for show and tell."

Suddenly they seemed to remember me, then looked at each other and laughed.

"Housewife! Housewife!" they sang, laughing.

After lunch, the teacher went around the room, having inquired of the class who had a parent coming and what they would be showing or telling.

"My mom's a secretary," said the girl sitting next to me. "She's going to show how fast she can type and then give us our words to take home."

Then it was my turn. "My mom is going to show you what you are."

The teacher, frowning. "What does that mean?"

"I don't know. It's what she told me to say."

Class snickering, slow blush filling my face.

Teacher again. "What does your mother do?"

"She can do a lot of things, but she almost always stays at home."

"So your mother is a homemaker."

"Maybe. I don't know what that word means. I never heard it before."

Low sing-song whispers from a corner of the room. "Housewife, housewife."

"Shhhh! Shhhh!" said the teacher, growing irritated. Then to me. "There's nothing wrong with being a homemaker, but you should ask your mother if there is anything special about what she does before she shows and tells. A lot of what homemakers do is unremarkable and the same. We don't want all the visiting mothers to say the same things."

I cried sometimes during naptime because I missed Mama so much. To help with this she had given me a toy version of her car that was exactly like it in most every way. I would lie on my mat and run the car over my chest and up and down my arms making a soft low sound like faraway thunder.

But then in my mind I could see her face at home and tell she was unhappy. My head began to throb and I would cry, softly and quietly, hot tears running over my temples and curving round my ears. It hurt my heart to know she was all by herself and unhappy. I wished I could be there with her. When the teacher grew angry and told me to stop crying, I always felt bad and apologized to her.

I wanted to stop crying, but I couldn't.

By the time my mother completed her doctorate at the Medical College of Virginia in the late 1960s, her research had made her one of the world's experts on the pineal gland, and so she received the rare professional privilege of a job offer from the school that had granted her terminal degree. She had been the only woman in her graduating class and, when she accepted the job, the only woman faculty member.

The first course she ever taught was in a large, sloping, concrete-floored lecture hall. One entered at the back and made a long descent to the stage, where stood two long chalkboards and a lab table.

Mama nearly always ran late so that on the first day of class, when she entered the auditorium at the rear, arms full of books and lecture notes, the students, over a hundred of them, all men, were assembled and waiting for her. Her lab coat distinguished her as a professor, but the expressions on their faces as they turned to consider her—disappointment, anxiety, dismissal—told the tale of their collective shock.

Whispers as she begins the slow descent to the stage, heels clicking steadily on the concrete. About halfway down someone launches a brief, piercing whistle—ancient trumpet sound of male admiration—applauded by sporadic laughs from his fellows.

Mama keeps walking.

At the bottom she mounts the two steps to the stage and walks to the lab table, where she sets down her books before looking up around the lecture hall, squinting slightly in the lights, taking in the vague sea of male faces.

She takes off her coat.

"That's right! Take it off!" cries an anonymous voice somewhere off to the left.

"Take it all off!" exclaims another on the opposite side of the room.

Burst of laughter from all sides.

Hands trembling slightly, Mama takes hold of her lecture notes and turns to write on one of the chalkboards.

"Nice ass!" a voice calls.

Then a hollow, slightly grating sound of motion and muffled laughter. Turning from the board Mama spies an empty jar rolling down the central aisle, students seated to the far sides of the auditorium half-rising from their seats so as to follow it with their heads. Picking up speed, the jar hits against the bottom stage step and careens to one side. More muffled laughter.

Mama turns back to the board and keeps writing, listing her key terms for the day.

A minute passes, etched sound of idea transformed into symbol.

Then, again, the rolling sound—closer, louder, varied in texture—as the jar rolls over the boards of the lecture stage. Mama turning just as it glances off her shoe. Loud laughter this time.

As the sound dies, Mama walks to the lab table and sets her chalk down. Then she takes off her glasses and sets them down too. As she looks back up and out over the indistinct audience a slow, warm smile forms on her face—the easy natural smile of a cheerleader or prom court princess, both of which she had been. She looks to one side of the auditorium and then to the other, hands on hips, smiling.

"Cutie!" calls a voice.

"Hottie!" says another.

Smile still intact, unwavering, Mama strides across the stage to where the jar lies resting. Hands still on hips, attitude of sensual affectation, she lifts her right foot, arches an eyebrow at her audience, then brings it down suddenly, heavily, air of the room pierced as glass shatters, echoes, jagged irregular pieces sliding across the stage in various directions.

Silence, pause, then the lonely sound of Mama's heels as she walks back to the table, puts on her glasses, and looks up around the lecture hall.

"Let's get to work, gentlemen."

Another time, lab, students about to begin dissecting cadavers, and Mama circulating about the room, prepping the class, heavy merged smell of chemical preservatives and disinfectant.

A tall student raising his hand, beckoning her toward his group's examination table. "Professor, our specimen here seems to have a problem."

Smirks from the others in the group and the nearby tables as Mama peers down at the cadaver to discover that on his forever limp penis someone has placed a condom.

She glances up at the student who has announced the anomaly, then looks around the table, noting the clenched jaws of his fellows, inner cheek linings held in check by clenched teeth. Then she smiles at them, her slow, warm, cheerleader smile, as if she too shares in the jest.

Leaning forward, she reaches across the table to take hold of the cadaver's penis, tugging it out to its sad, unerect fullness.

"Hell yeah!" exclaims a student in another part of the room.

Then Mama's other hand in motion, bearing her scalpel. Sudden, deft flash of metal in the fluorescent light and her hand comes away with the leaden member.

Sharp, collective intake of air from multiple mouths and a couple of audible groans.

"This little thing isn't relevant or useful for this lab practical, or even to the semester's curriculum," she announces in her lecture voice, shaking the hand that holds it for emphasis. "It's just not useful."

With that she tosses it in the tableside biowaste container and moves on to inspect the cadaver on the next table, students falling back from her, two of them stumbling over each other, almost falling, as if some new invisible force surrounds this woman's body, emanating outward on all sides.

When she quit she took everything her grant money had purchased: microscopes, vials, petri dishes, burners, hamster cages, protein formulae, a cross-section composite of a fetal pig, even a human skeleton.

"Surely," said the department chair, "you are not taking the skeleton. It will be of little use beyond the academic community."

"He goes with me," my mother said, "And if I were you, I wouldn't be too sure of anything."

"There is . . . a class of monsters who might live, but which would always remain freaks."
--Charles Sumner Bacon, "A Symposium on Obstetrical Abnormalities" (1916)

Sitting on a shelf in a little windowless supply room just off one of the dissection labs was the Medical College's collection of genetic mutations: a dozen infants and fetuses afloat in large, clear glass containers of formaldehyde. I used to dream about them when I was younger.

The variations of these beings were obvious and subtle, shocking and secretive. Several were possessed of different degrees of encephaloceles, the meninges protruding from their heads' occipital region in a number of different shapes and geometric designs. What would that feel like? One was visited with holoprosencephaly, its nostril displaced and its optical qualities all fused together into a great single orb. What might such an eye have seen? And an instance of doubling to balance this cyclopean collapse: an infant possessed of one body and two heads, the result of duplication of the neural tube. What would these heads have said to each other? What would they have thought?

Later, in college, reading on my own, I would come across a poem about a baby that was half-child, half-lamb. "In a museum in Atlanta," it reads, "Way back in a corner somewhere/There's this thing that's only half/Sheep like a woolly baby/Pickled in alcohol . . . ." I thought so much of the poem that I resolved to study writing under the man who had created it, hoping perhaps to develop the powers to commit my own real and imagined monsters to paper—to afford them a kind of immortality through my rendering, which might also, in turn—I hoped—provide me with something at last from them. "Are we," asks my old literary master, "Because we remember, remembered/In the terrible dust of museums?"

When I dreamed of them, they would move, but they never left their containers. Their meninges would pulsate, throb, with life. The mouths of the two heads would take turns opening and closing, bubbles emerging into the vat's closed liquid world, traveling upward. And then, very slowly, as if awakening even as I slept, the lid of the great single eye would draw back and the enormous orb would regard me—neither warmly nor coldly, but with some vague aspect of feeling—watching.

Little lamb, who made thee?
Dost thou know who made thee?

I suppose they did look monstrous and terrible, but I was never afraid of them. They were my friends.

If they could have smiled at me, they would have. And I would have smiled back.

The pineal gland is situated in the very center of the brain, in a tiny little cave-like enclosure beyond and above the pituitary gland, and directly behind the eyes—to which it is attached by the third ventricle.

It controls the biorhythms of the body, and though head injuries may activate it, it typically is triggered by changes in light, working in harmony with the hypothalamus gland to direct our emotions, thirst, hunger, sexual desire, and the biological clock that determines aging.

The Greeks considered the pineal gland our site of connection to The Realms of Thought. Descartes thought it the seat of the soul—the place where the interaction between the intellect and the body takes place. Myth and legend from a time before science? Even now there are those who refer to it as "The Third Eye."

Sitting together in a pasture meadow, patched quilt spread out beneath us, Mama's arm resting across my shoulders. Afternoon sun of spring casting long shadows of tree branches upon the ground, where the breeze flutters slightly the new blades of grass.

A blue bird, landing less than a foot from my foot, chirping and turning its tiny head sideways to regard me. Then he hops—three short, plump, quick hops—to the end of my shoe and bends forward, craning his neck to examine it.

I whisper something and he searches my face before hopping onto my shoe, glancing at me again, then launching himself, soaring up and then back behind us, toward the trees that cast shadows.

I turn back from the bird's path to discover Mama watching me intently.

"Why did the bird come so close, Mama?"

"Animals can tell things about other creatures."

"You mean just by looking?"

"More than just looking. We can't really explain what they do because we are not them."

"The little bird could tell about me."

"That's right. He could tell about you. That's why he came so close."

I lean my head against her and as I do she draws back her arm and then lets it fall, trailing her forefinger down my back, tapping each ridge of my spine as if marking a paper. Then the hand comes back up, fingers absently playing about my hair like butterflies.

"You are very nearly perfect," she says. "Just how I imagined you would be."

She draws me to her. "My precious creation."

After a while I pull away and look up at her. "Mama, I can tell about you. You're sad."

"I'm not sad, honey. I was only thinking."

"Does thinking make you sad?"

Short laugh. "It can, I suppose, but I'm not sad. You're here with me and when we're together I can never be sad."

Silence from me and she smiles. "Now, what are you thinking about?"

"I was thinking about the little bird who could tell about me. Do you think he'll be OK when it gets dark? I wish I could help him."

"I think he'll be OK, but it's good you want to help him. You must always help creatures and people if they need help and deserve it."

"Why do I have to help people? Who's going to help me?"

"When you get bigger you aren't going to need help, but because you will have a powerful ability to help people, you must always do so. You needn't help everyone. There are some who won't want it and some who won't deserve it, but you will be able to tell who they are. And remember that when you do help, it's the help they don't realize that helps the most."

"You mean the secret help?"

"That's right. The secret help."

"What if I don't know what to do?"

"It is part of a being's existence to make mistakes, but you have to be brave and try. Even when there are many people against you. That is what is called courage. Do you understand?"

"I think so."

"Then promise me you'll do it."

"I will, Mama. I promise."

Mama was always running behind. Usually it was because she had stayed up too late reading or perhaps had lingered too long in bed the following morning with her coffee and books. Sometimes if I was upstairs in my room she would call to me and tell me to go get her a refill to spare her having to get up.

She claimed she hated going anywhere, but she loved to drive. Rushing to town, hopelessly late, well over the speed limit, she was happy.

"Always go into a curve slow and come out of it fast," she would say, stabbing the accelerator as the road broke straight.

And, me, next to her, equally happy, standing on the floorboard, hands on the dashboard, peering out over it, wide-eyed, smiling. "Come out fast, Mama! Come out fast!"

Sometimes, if the road curved to the left, I would fall against the door. And if the curve to the right was a hard one, I would tumble over into her lap and lie there laughing, peering up into her face until she laughed too.

She kept the skeleton in a corner of the upstairs cedar closet. It was easy to miss on account of all the various things clinging to different parts of it: winter caps stacked upon its smooth head, heavy old shirts and frayed coats flung over its shoulders, an assortment of Christmas ornaments hanging from its lower ribs, and a child-sized basketball resting in its pelvis. The piled hats leaned slightly to one side, affording the skull a jaunty aspect, while the rough clothing drooping from the shoulders hung irregularly—not unlike rock-hewn prehistoric furs from some distant cold-climate predecessor of us. The basketball resting in the midsection suggested an impossible pregnancy, and the bone-suspended ornaments could not help but appear festive, speaking, it seemed to me, of some secret grisly truth yet to be celebrated. A big steel rod rose out of a metal base resting on rollers and ran upward through the spinal column before terminating in the skull, creating the illusion of a body somehow hovering in air of its own volition, feet dangling three or four inches above the floor.

Despite the novelty of the thing's presence, the skeleton really was just another item in storage—something put away, half-forgotten. Sometimes when I was helping Mama in the closet, she would address the occupant with "And how are we today, my good man?" or "Excuse us, sir" or "Don't mind us, old friend." She always seemed happy to see him—an acquaintance from another time; a fondly remembered ally from a war long over.

I would visit him sometimes when I was upstairs alone, rush of cedar as I swung forth the door and flipped on the light. Carefully I would place my little hand against his, studying the contrast, and then pressing each of my fingers against a corresponding fleshless digit.

Even at that age I did not need my mother to tell me this was what I would be some day. That it was what lay in store. Some fundamental cognition knew. And it was comforting in a way, a privilege, to have this visual testament available day or night, close at hand and always the same, which seemed to say, "Beneath all the motion and coating of life, here is what you are."

I have no recollection of the truth of this ever troubling me. Perhaps it had something to do with the fact he did not seem to mind it so much himself. Whenever I opened the door, his expression was the same. He was always smiling.

Parent Show and Tell Day and Mama running even later than usual, the time for heading to school coming and going with her propped against her pillows, briskly flipping pages while sipping at her coffee.

"I'll just take you when it gets to be time for my visit," she said when I checked on her. "We'll visit school together. Now go and get me another cup."

Lunchtime passed and I was out in front of the house feeding butterflies, tips of my fingers all sticky with sugar water, when finally I heard her calling me. Upward patchwork flutter as I blew gently on my forefinger to dismiss my guest before turning to run around back of the house.

At first I did not think the woman standing next to the car was Mama, the figure in the sleeveless white spring dress and black heels and sunglasses appearing more like someone out of one of the women's magazines I had seen in doctors' offices. I hesitated, gawking. But then she smiled and waved for me to come on, and I knew it was her.

"Let's go," she called. "We're late!"

Spray of rocks and scattering of panicked chickens as we plowed up the driveway, windows all the way down and Mama humming softly to herself a song I did not know, while behind us, on the back seat, a third passenger lay sprawled.

Faster than ever, around the curves and over the straightaways, occasional dry click of bone from the back when the swaying of the car forced an arm or leg to adjust itself. Trio of bodies reacting in unison—dead or alive, no matter—moving as commanded by the physics of motion. Smiles on all our faces.

Then glare of blue lights in the rearview mirror and blast of a siren.

Me, pivoting, knees on the seat, chin atop the headrest, peering backward. "The police, Mama! The police!"

Silently we slow and drift onto the shoulder to the tune of crunched gravel, engine relaxing into a low, steady growl.

Me, staring back at the man in the hat and sunglasses as he considers our car before glancing down. Then, door opening, he rises from his vehicle, sunglasses removed: a tall gangly fellow, polished black belt and holster set in relief against a garb of brown and tan.

And Mama, June sun smiling down into the car upon her, pretty in her sleeveless dress, slender arms rigidly extended, hands on the steering wheel, knuckles white, daring the road ahead with a fixed stare, teeth set to grind, eyes shifting to the rearview mirror as the man approaches.

Me, watching as he comes on, slight sway to his stride, careless gaze resting on the back of Mama's head, ignoring me altogether. Watching still as he reaches the tail end of the car and leans forward, easy look drifting into the back seat—where something catches it, knocks it askew, then empties it of itself. Eyes jerking dumbly from the prone form to the back of Mama's head, before discerning her gaze in the rearview mirror, sunglasses removed, boring into his, fixing him in place. He stands there frozen, as if changed to stone, face slack-jawed, blood drained from it.

"We are late for our school presentation, officer," she calls back to him without turning.

The man, stammering, taking a few tentative steps toward the front of the car.

"It is a matter of vital importance," she goes on, as if lecturing. "We cannot afford further delay. Much is at stake which cannot be made evident to you, and I do not have time to explain."

The officer, a local deputy, draws even with her window, making his best effort to recover himself. "Are you some kind of doctor?"

Mama placing her forearm on the door, smiling

up at him her warm, slow smile. "I am indeed a *kind* of doctor," she says, "insofar as I am a woman, concerned with restoring or manipulating human health through the highly detailed study, diagnosis, and treatment of the human body."

She glances over at me and smiles her true smile before turning back to him. "Beneath your clothes and your flesh, you are not very different from that fellow in the back seat. Have you ever thought about that? I mean *really* thought about it? Such is the nature of most all people on this earth: so few come to realize or even bother to think about the fundamental nature of themselves."

Her smile hardens, then lapses into a line and she stares up at him. "We are going to show them what they are."

The deputy, still quite pale, nodding slowly and agreeably, wholly acquiescent even as he comprehends nothing. "Mam," he says at last, "I think you know what your business is, and I do believe I am going to let you get about it right now."

With that he turns quickly and walks briskly back to his car, hand slipping slightly on the door handle as he seeks to jerk it open—to get inside, away, anywhere else.

And Mama, back out on the road before the deputy is even in his seat, driving as fast as before, faster even, dials on the dash a confusion of vibrating needles, grinning at the long white highway lines devoured beneath us.

Sliding to a stop between two buses in the circular school parking lot, not far from the main entrance. Car doors open, front seats leaned forward, Mama motioning me to climb into the back.

Gesturing at the skeleton's base. "Help me lift him, son."

Me, curiously strong for a child my age, grasping him by the rollers and heaving upward and forward, slipping a bit as I step out onto the gravel, banging a femur against the door.

"Careful now," says Mama, her steady hands clenched about his collarbone.

Then, me, letting down the base and together— me pushing and Mama pulling—bringing him upright. He sways slightly before leveling out between us, blinding white of bone and flashing metal in the end-of-school-year sun.

We roll him slowly, haltingly, over the gravel lot toward the entrance, me pushing while bracing the backs of his legs, and Mama steadying him, arm about his waist in the attitude a nurse will adopt while guiding a frail elderly patient.

Through the heavy school doors to discover emptiness inside, an industrial fan, nearly as tall as our companion, the sole occupant, blowing at the far end of a dim forlorn hallway, caressing our damp foreheads with warm air. Rolling him down the corridor, shut crayoned doors of classrooms passing on either side, the going much easier on the polished smooth floor though a wheel squeaks slightly, piercing occasionally the droning refrain of mechanically pushed air.

As we turn a corner a janitor steps forth from his closet, then, noticing us, retreats wide-eyed back into it, drawing the door shut before him, water bucket sloshing—lapsing into a motionless silhouette behind beveled glass.

Arriving at last at the door to my classroom, student roster hanging on it with stars of different colors attending each name. Only a few next to mine, all of a lesser hue.

Mama absorbing this data in a glance, then hand on my shoulder, gentle and firm, moving me out of the way. "Stand aside, son."

Door flung open, swinging inward, and in rolls the skeleton, Mama pushing him from behind, teacher and students frozen in their places, mouths rounded and agape, eyes nearly as large. The skeleton coming forward, passing between the main center rows of desks and up to the very head of the room. He stops before the teacher and Mama steps out from behind, appraising the woman with a frank stare, looking her up and down. The teacher had always seemed to me so large and frightening, but next to Mama—so tall and pretty and smart in her heels and spring dress—the teacher looked small and old and plain. I felt sorry for her. Her throat moved and she shuddered suddenly—at Mama or the skeleton I couldn't tell which.

When Mama turned to address the class she rolled the skeleton about with her so that they turned together, gracefully, in unison, like dancers or skaters, the teacher falling back away from them, like a lesser actress abandoning the stage.

Then Mama began speaking to the students and as she did a strange glow came over her which I had never seen before. "I am sorry we are late today for show and tell," she says, "but real learning never runs on time and for us I hope you will make an exception."

Quick glance at the teacher, who nods uncertainly, before continuing. "I believe my son informed you that I would show you what you are." Heads swiveling briefly to where I stand at the back of the class.

"Well," she continues, "here you are. Here is what you all are beneath your clothes and your skin. Look at your arm. Look at your hand. Then think about that for a minute. Think about it."

Students extending their arms, holding out their palms before them.

"Your human skeleton, this thing inside you, is very strong and very hard, yet it is relatively light. I bet your mothers weigh you sometimes. We like to know how big you are getting. In a man like this one who weighed maybe 160 pounds the skeleton is only 30 pounds.

"And it is perfectly adapted for locomotion and manipulation," she goes on, lifting the skeleton's forearm so that its elbow joint flexes. "See?"

Widening eyes at this.

"Now, it is our spines that are responsible for our upright posture," she says, running her hand down the skeleton's back. "Because we stand upright, we are able to use our hands in order to manipulate our environment. We reach out and we *change* things.

"An adult human skeleton consists of 206 bones altogether which are divided into two principal divisions: the axial skeleton and the appendicular skeleton. The axial forms the long axis of the body and it includes the bones of the skull, vertebral column, breastbone, and rib cage. The appendicular consists of the bones of the upper and lower extremities, the shoulder girdle, and the hip girdle."

As Mama points to each bone grouping in succession, naming each again, the students watch her finger, then look down at the corresponding places on their bodies.

"I could show and tell about this forever," Mama says, "but the best showers and tellers care about what other people want to know. I am interested in you all. What do you want to know?"

Stunned silence, then a lethargic stirring as if awakening from the same powerful dream.

"Is it a boy or a girl?" a boy asks.

"He was a man," says Mama, "a very old man. You can tell he was old a lot of different ways, but all of you can see how he's missing some teeth and the ones that are left are all ground down from use."

"Why is that?" another boys asks. "Where did he come from?"

"Southeast Asia," replies Mama. "I can tell because of his bone structure and cranial development."

A girl. "Where is that?"

"On the other side of the world," says Mama. "The people there are much poorer than you and I and don't always get to eat their meals. Think about that for a minute. What if you missed your dinner for a whole week? Just imagine how hungry you would be. This fellow was hungry a lot of the time. His bones say so."

The teacher, off to the side, rigid and frowning.

Another girl. "How did he come all the way here?"

"Sometimes when people die their bodies get sent to scientists so they can be studied. That is what

I used to be: a scientist, a *woman* scientist. I studied bodies so that I could learn about how to work on the ones that are alive and make them better."

Students staring at Mama in wonder, a pair of girls peering uncertainly across the aisle at each other, possessed suddenly of new eyes.

"I like talking to you all," she says, smiling a warm, slow smile, and they all smile back at her. "Now for the real fun. Who wants to touch him?"

Eruption of hands and a piping chorus of "Me! Me! Me!" Bodies abandoning their desks, pressing forward as a body. My little classmates, weaving around the skeleton in a frenzy of fascination, quick touches from small forefingers—one girl reaching up to grab a bottom rib, then lifting her shirt to poke at her own.

And me, apart from the others, with eyes only for my mother: towering above the swirl of motion, commanding the classroom, beaming down upon the children, showing them themselves.

Mark Edmundson

The World According to Falwell

I teach at the University of Virginia, and not far from me, down Route 29 in Lynchburg—whence the practice of lynching some claim, gets its name—is the church of Jerry Falwell. Falwell teaches "the word of God," the literal, unarguable truth as it's revealed to him in the Bible and as it must be understood by all heaven-bound Christians.

For some time, I thought that we at the University of Virginia had nothing consequential to do with the Reverend Falwell. Occasionally, I'd get a book through interlibrary loan from Falwell's Liberty University; sometimes the inside cover contained a warning to the pious suggesting that though this volume might be the property of the Liberty University library, its contents, insofar as they contradict the Bible (which means the Bible according to Falwell) were of no particular value.

It's said that when a certain caliph was on the verge of burning the great library at Alexandria, scholars fell on their knees in front of him and begged him to relent. "There are two kinds of books here," the caliph purportedly said. "There are those that contradict the Koran-they are blasphemous. There are those that corroborate the Koran-they are superfluous." So: "Burn the library." Given the possibilities for fundamentalist literary criticism that the caliph opened up, it's a good thing that Liberty has a library at all.

Thomas Jefferson, the University of Virginia's founder, was a deist, maybe something more scandalous than that, the orthodox of Virginia used to whisper. The architecture of my university's central grounds, all designed by Jefferson, is emphatically secular, based on Greek and Roman models. In fact, the Rotunda, once the university's library, is designed in homage to the Roman Pantheon, a temple to the twelve chief pagan gods. Where the statues of those gods stand in the Pantheon, there, in the Rotunda library, were books. Books were Jefferson's deities, invested with powers of transport and transformation equal to anything the ancient gods possessed. As soon as they saw the new university, local divines went apoplectic. Where was the church? Unlike Princeton and Harvard, the state university didn't have a Christian house of worship at its center. From pulpits all over Virginia, ministers threatened the pagan enclave with ruin from above. In 1829, the Episcopal bishop William Meade predicted the university's ruin, because, as he put it, the "Almighty is angry" about the Rotunda. (It's probably only fair to report that in 1895 the Rotunda did burn down.)

Jefferson—deist (maybe worse), scientist, cosmopolitan—seems to have believed that the best way to deal with religion was to banish it, formally, from the university, and instead to teach the useful arts of medicine, commerce, law, and the rest. The design of my university declares victory over what the radicals of the Enlightenment would have called superstition, and what most Americans currently call faith or spirituality. And we honor Jefferson now by, in effect, rendering unto Falwell that which is Falwell's.

In fact, we—and I don't mean only at the University of Virginia, I mean humanists in general—have entered into an implied bargain with Falwell and other American promulgators of faith, most of whom have much more to recommend them than the Prophet of Lynchburg. They do the soul-crafting. They administer the spiritual education. They address the hearts of our students, and in some measure of the nation at large. We preside over the minds. We shape intelligences; we train the faculties (and throw in more than a little entertainment on the side).

In other words, we teachers strike an unspoken agreement with religion and its dispensers. They do their work, we do ours.

But isn't that the way it should be? Isn't religion private? Spirituality, after all, is everyone's personal affair; it shouldn't be the substance of college education; it should be passed over in silence. What professor would have the bad taste to puncture the walls of his students' privacy, to invade their inner lives, by asking them uncomfortable questions about ultimate values?

Well, it turned out, me. I decided that I was, in a certain sense, going to take my cue from religion. After all, I got into teaching for the same reason, I suspect, that many people did: because I thought it was a high-stakes affair, a pursuit in which souls are won and lost.

"How do you imagine God?" If you are going to indulge in embarrassing behavior, if you're going to make your students "uncomfortable," why not go all the way? This question has moved to the center of many of my classes—not classes in religion, but classes in Shakespeare, in Romantic poetry, in major nineteenth-century novels. That is, the embarrassing question begins courses with which, according to Jefferson, according to Falwell and other, more tempered advocates of faith, and according to the great majority of my colleagues in the humanities, it has absolutely nothing to do.

What kind of answers do I get? Often marvelous ones. After the students who are disposed to walk out have, sometimes leaving an editorial sigh hanging in the air, and after there's been a weekend for reflection, answers come forth.

Some of the accounts are on the fluffy side. I've learned that God is love and only love; I've heard that God is Nature; that God is light; that God is all the goodness in the universe. I hear tales about God's interventions into the lives of my students, interventions that save them from accidents, deliver them from sickness while others fall by the wayside. There's a whole set of accounts that are on the all-benevolent side-smiling, kindly, but also underramified, insufficiently thought-out. If God is all things, or abides in all things, then what is the source of evil? (By now, it's clear to the students that bad taste is my game; already I'm getting a little by way of indulgence.) A pause, then an answer, sometimes not a bad one. The most memorable exponent of smiling faith was a woman named Catherine, who called her blend of creamy benevolence—what else?—Catherinism.

But I respected Catherine for speaking as she did, for unfolding herself bravely. In general, humanities classes, where questions of ultimate belief should be asked and answered all the time, have nothing to do with those questions. It takes courage to make this first step, and to speak candidly about yourself.

Some of the responses are anything but under-elaborated. These tend to come from my orthodoxly religious students, many of whom are well trained, maybe overtrained, in the finer points of doctrine. I get some hardcore believers. But in general it wouldn't be fair to call them Falwell's children, because they're often among the most thoughtful students in the class. They, unlike the proponents of the idea that God is light and that's all you need to know in life, are interested in delving into major questions. They care about understanding the source of evil. They want to know what it means to live a good life. And though they're rammed with doctrine, they're not always addicted to dogma. There's often more than a little room for doubt. Even if their views are sometimes rock solid, they don't mind seeing them besieged. Because given their interests, they're glad that "this discussion is not about any chance question, but about the way one should live."

Final Narratives

Religion is the right place to start a humanities course, for a number of reasons, even if what we're going on to do is to read the novels of Henry James. One of them is that religion is likely to be a major element in my students' Final Narratives, a term I adapt from Richard Rorty. A Final Narrative (Rorty actually says Final Vocabulary; I modify him slightly) involves the ultimate set of terms that we use to confer value on experience. It's where our principles are manifest. When someone talks feelingly about the Ten Commandments, or the Buddha's Four Noble Truths, or the innate goodness of human beings, or about all human history being the history of class conflict, then, in all likelihood, she has revealed something close to the core of her being. She's touched on her ultimate terms of commitment, the point beyond which argument and analysis are unlikely to go, at least very quickly. Rorty puts it this way: "All human beings carry about a set of words which they employ to justify their actions, their beliefs, and their lives. These are the words in which we formulate praise of our friends and contempt for our enemies, our long-term projects, our deepest self-doubts and our highest hopes. They are the words in which we tell, sometimes prospectively and sometimes retrospectively, the story of our lives."

Rorty's word "final" is ironic, or potentially so. His sense is that a "final" language ought to be anything but final. He believes that we ought to be constantly challenging, testing, refining, and if need be overthrowing our ultimate terms and stories, replacing them with others that serve us better. Certain people, says Rorty, are "always aware that the terms in which they describe themselves are subject to change, always aware of the contingency and fragility of their final vocabularies, and thus of their selves." But Rorty believes that most people never stray far from their initial narratives, the values that they're imprinted with while they're growing up. Most of us stay at home.

Rorty calls people capable of adopting new languages "ironists," because they inflect even their most fervent commitments with doubt. It's possible, they know, that what today they hold most intimately true will be replaced tomorrow by other, better ways of seeing and saying things. They comprehend what Rorty likes to call the contingency of their own current state.

Appreciating this contingency is very close to appreciating one's own mortality. That is, Rorty's ironists are people who know that they exist in time because it is time and the changes it brings that can make their former terminologies and their former selves obsolete. Terms that serve your purposes one day will not necessarily do so the next. The ironists' willingness to change narratives, expand their circles of self, is something of a brave act, in part because all awareness of existence in time is awareness of death. To follow the ironists' path is to admit to mortality.

In trying to make contact with my students' Final Narratives, I ask about more than religion. I ask about how they imagine the good life. I ask, sometimes, how they picture their lives in ten years if all turns out for the best. I want to know what they hope to achieve in politics, in their professions, in family life, in love. Occasionally, I ask how they conceive of Utopia, the best of all possible worlds, or of Dystopia, the worst. But usually, for me, the matter of religion is present, a central part of the question.

There is nothing new about beginning a humanistic inquiry in this way. At the start of The Republic, Socrates asks his friends what they think justice is. And for Socrates, justice is the public and private state conducive to the good life. The just state and the just soul are mirror images of each other, comparably balanced. Socrates is quickly answered. Thrasymachus, aggressively, sometimes boorishly, insists that justice is the interest of the stronger. Socrates isn't put off by Thrasymachus, not at all. For Socrates recognizes that getting his students to reveal themselves as they are, or appear to themselves to be, is the first step in giving them the chance to change.

Posing the question of religion and the good life allows students to become articulate about who and

what they are. They often react not with embarrassment or anxiety, but with surprise and pleasure, as
if no one has ever thought to ask them such a question and they've never posed it to themselves.

But beginning here, with religion, also implies
a value judgment on my part—the judgment that the
most consequential questions for an individual life
(even if one is, as I am, a longtime agnostic) are related to questions of faith. I also believe, for reasons
I will get to later, that at this historical juncture, the
matter of belief is crucial to our common future.

Most professors of the humanities have little interest in religion as a field of live options. Most of us
have had our crises of faith early, if we've had them
at all, and have adopted, almost as second nature,
a secular vision of life. Others keep their religious
commitments separate from their pedagogy, and
have for so long that they're are hardly aware of it.
But what is old to the teacher is new to the student.
This question of belief matters greatly to the young,
or at least it does in my experience. Asking it can
break through the ideologies of training and enter-
taining. Beneath that veneer of cool, students are
full of potent questions; they want to know how to
navigate life, what to be, what to do. Matters of faith
and worldliness are of great import to our students
and by turning away from them, by continuing our
treaty with the dispensers of faith where we tutor
the mind and they take the heart and spirit, we do
our students injustice.

We secular professors often forget that America
is a religion-drenched nation. Ninety percent of
us believe that God knows and loves us personally, as individuals. More than the citizens of any
other postindustrial nation, we Americans attend
church—and synagogue, and mosque. We affirm
faith. We elect devout, or ostensibly devout, believers to the White House; recent presidents have been
born-again Christians. Probably one cannot be
elected president of the United States—cannot be
our Representative Man—without professing strong
religious faith. The struggle over whether America's

future will be sacred or secular, or a mix of the two, is critical to our common future.

Some may well disagree with me about the centrality of religious matters, matters of ultimate belief, in shaping a true literary education. I teach in the South, one of the more religiously engaged parts of the nation, after all. Fine. But I think the point stands nonetheless. Get to your students' Final Narratives, and your own; seek out the defining beliefs. Uncover central convictions about politics, love, money, the good life. It's there that, as Socrates knew, real thinking starts.

Margaret Gibson

The Queen of Hearts

Shetland sweaters were a must, but they were expensive, especially at Steve and Anna's, the select little shop in Westhampton where St. Catherine's girls bought their clothes. My mother rummaged in an attic trunk and found a sweater, dusky rose in color, with the large yarn look of a Shetland, and she gave it to me. She had worn it in college, she said proudly, and since I was tall, it just might fit me. Wearing it and my fashionable new shoes—clunky boats of brilliant white leather with saddles of brown and broad white laces—I made my way toward my assigned desk in the Middle School's study hall, avoiding the ring-binder notebooks that edged into the narrow aisle as a few intent girls finished their homework assignments. Study Hall was silent at all times, except for morning announcements and morning chapel. I could hear the scrape of pencils, the dull friction of erasers.

The seventh graders sat one behind another in long rows that abutted matching rows of eighth graders. My desk was next to eighth grader Armistead Merriweather, to whom I had never spoken because I only saw her in Study Hall. Armistead was as exotic to me as a movie star. Her skin looked velvety, tawny. Hers were the largest, most liquid brown eyes I had ever seen. She had fingernails—polished—and a little gold ring. Her clothes came from Steve and Anna's. Our teachers counted on their authority to keep the silence in study hall, but it also helped that to a seventh grader, most eighth graders appeared to be unapproachably mature and experienced. I wouldn't have dared begin a conversation with an eighth grader. When I looked at my seventh grade classmates, I saw the bodies of girls still coltish and unsure. The eighth graders wore their sweaters and skirts with grace and style. Lipstick wasn't allowed at school, but we knew that many older girls had a tube of lipstick hidden away in their pencil cases. Hair combed and lipstick ready for a quick swipe once they were released onto Grove Avenue at three o'clock, the eighth graders gathered at Doc White's pharmacy on the corner of Grove and Maple, to talk with the boys from St. Christopher's. If a boy had a crush on you, he was "snowed." From the bus stop on the opposite corner, I watched the crowd at Doc White's, and like most of my friends, I was gawky, tongue-tied, and envious.

In field hockey, an eighth grader's body followed Miss Fleet's instructions with apparently flawless ease. I stumbled over my stick, failing to send the ball with a confident crack to its destination in the field. How did they do it—Kitty Anderson, Marty Davenport, Lucy Day, Isabel Rawlings? In their short yellow uniforms with bloomers, they couldn't have looked more comical, and yet, given their skill, they managed to give off a gritty allure. Studying them from a distance, I imagined my own body into existence, burgeoning toward a maturity that wouldn't have to think about itself. Eighth grade was the future close at hand, beheld but not grasped.

With a swift, side-long glance I studied Armistead Merriweather. She was perfect.

Perfect, but not a top student or a top athlete. Perfect, but with a most peculiar manner during morning prayers, the time I had my best look at her. During chapel at our desks, I couldn't take my eyes off Armistead, even though my head was bowed, and my mind supposedly focused on an omniscient and omnipotent God with the same concentration I gave to ungovernable fractions. Together, both grades prayed what we had memorized from *The Book of Common Prayer*, reciting by heart the required General Confession: *Almighty and most*

Merciful Father, We have erred and strayed from Thy ways like lost sheep. We have followed too much the devices and desires of our own hearts. We have offended against Thy holy laws. As she spoke the words softly, Armistead's head bent so low to her desk that her mouth met the wood. Her full, generous mouth opened slightly, seeming to kiss the desk, an open-mouthed kiss that skimmed the surface, not quite kissing, but what else was it? I heard small gasps of breath. *We have left undone those things which we ought to have done. And we have done those things which we ought not to have done; And there is no health in us.* The desk was a dark mirror. I could almost see Armistead's warm breath upon it. Was she kissing herself? An imagined boy? God? Now her mouth opened wider and her lips rested on the wood, murmuring *Spare Thou those, O God, who confess their faults.*

I held my breath as Armistead's mouth married her faults to the study hall desk, her lips wet, her eyes closed, her soft hair fallen over her forehead—she was the carnal embodiment of the words we had recited in the call to prayer: *O Lord, open Thou our lips.* To which we had responded, *And our mouth shall show forth Thy praise.* Whether it was praise or plea, Douglas Noel—and all of us—concluded the confession: *That we may hereafter live a godly, righteous, and sober life, To the glory of Thy holy name, Amen.* As we straightened in our chairs, Armistead looked at me and smiled, gathering her books, making ready to sprint out of study hall to class. Did she know I adored her? Spent from the labor of my attention to her praying, I smiled shyly back and ducked my head inside the slant-top desk to gather my notebook and pencils.

Miss Hood, our history teacher, was a fairy godmother in tweeds, her body a tidy little barrel on bird stilt legs. She wore lace-up shoes that seemed too large for her little body. She wouldn't hurt a fly, if one judged from the sweetness of her face or, less charitably, from the wavering warble of her speaking voice. And yet there was a ferocity to occasional remarks and predictions. "If your parents think the Russians are bad," she warned, tapping a map of the Middle East, "let them look to the desert. *Here* is where the future wars will be fought." She lowered her voice an octave. "Oil," she said, and the heating pipes in the old bungalow, one of the three original buildings, knocked and hissed.

Melissa Banning dutifully wrote down the word *oil* in her notebook. Cookie Lewis was still my best friend, but it seemed as if the classroom seating assignments in Middle School had been designed to part friends and scatter cliques. I saw Cookie only from across the room, rows of classmates between us. By chance or design I was placed next to Melissa Banning in History, Biology, and Math. I was getting used to showing my grades to her at her request when our papers were returned, and she occasionally phoned me at home. Among the first in our class to wear saddle shoes and pleated wool skirts, she seemed to know everyone and even had a friend among the eighth graders, Meade Davidson, for whom the study hall had risked Miss Thruston's ire by breaking into applause when Meade emerged from the bathroom with a triumphant grin which every eighth grader and many in the seventh knew how to interpret. Slight and underdeveloped, Meade was the last in her class to menstruate. Everyone knew she was waiting for Mother Nature to bestow on her the physical maturity which most seventh graders had attained. Her waiting was a physical trial, each month another chapter in a series of suspenseful moments. Her triumphant grin could therefore mean one thing only: finally! Her friends applauded, then everyone else did, Miss Thruston sputtered, shook the wattles of her chin and grew red-faced. "Girls!" she cried. In her maiden outrage and Victorian body, she resembled a hen turkey. "Girls!" Meade, with her childish body and a sophistication of manner that was second nature to her, merely bowed, blew kisses, and smiled.

Melissa Banning, graceful only on the athletic

field, was gangly and unformed. In the classroom she twirled a bit of hair with one hand and took notes with the other. She bit the side of her cheek during tests and moved the leg crossed over her knee up and down like a manic wood saw. Often chosen as class captain of the Gold team in our Gold-White rivalries, this year Melissa had been elected president of our class.

"Be careful," prim Kate Pinckney cautioned, as we rode home on the #15 bus. She had noticed Melissa's attentions to me but would say no more than those two words. "Ask Susan Abbot," she finally offered, closing the conversation firmly. But Susan was not in any of my classes; she lived on Patterson Avenue—too far to visit after school—and she was close to being another one of the outsiders in the class, those mysteriously unpopular, disregarded girls like Patty Wells, Shirley Fairgrieve, invisible Mary Hogue, or Annie Coleman. I tried to figure it out. Was it that Shirley's voice was too shrill, her body too scrawny? Was it that Annie always said the wrong thing and wrung her hands? Was it that Patty's clothes were too small for her and Mary's skin so freckled that she slunk into the shadows for camouflage? Their lack of popularity hung on them like a faint sour odor, untraceable but persistent. They were solitaries, belonging to no group, no clique.

I thought of the scatter of stars in the night sky, some clustered, some far flung and solitary. I thought of jack rocks—the jacks thrown up and spilled randomly on the floor. Some jacks fell into clusters, some skidded off alone, too remote from the others to be gathered in. Considering that I was a relative newcomer to this class at St. Catherine's, I was grateful for my friendship with Cookie Lewis, and I protected it.

Was I going to the slumber party at Bear Island? Melissa wanted to know as we changed classes. *Good*, she replied, when I nodded. Bear Island was the country home of Cookie's grandparents, the Parrish's. Cookie and her cousin Kathy Parrish were hosting a sleep-over, and Cookie had invited, predictably, her neighbor Sally Everson and me. Kathy had invited Melissa, Page Fitzgerald, Mary Tyler, and Corbin White—popular girls chosen from the athletic, brainy clusters in the class. It was my first slumber party with a large group of girls, and I was excited and a little nervous, more accustomed to the intimate and nearly familial weekends at the Lewis' house, our rituals of movies during the afternoon and card games at night, and when possible spying on Cookie's older sister Barbara, home from Hollins Abroad. "Baa" was as forbidding and irascible as brother Kent was pliable and sweet.

Kent had to cross through Cookie's bedroom to get to his own. Saturday nights, he would knock, wait, and knock again as Cookie and I leapt into bed, pulling the covers to our collarbones. As Kent, a tenth grader, crossed the room and entered the sanctum of his own room, my cheeks glowed hot, a heat that gradually reached what must have been my heart. Clearly, I was "snowed." Snowed and terrified that Cookie would guess it. Had she known, our friendship might have altered, and I knew that rompish, shy, awkward Cookie needed me as much as I needed her, lest we both be loners to whom no one talked at lunch. The years would pass, I imagined, following the movie in my mind, and Kent would notice me. We'd marry, and Cookie would be my sister until death parted us.

I liked the expression "snowed." It didn't snow in Richmond often, but after gray skies and the rush of snow came winter's clean bright air and a changed world. Snow was beautiful in the air, treacherous underfoot, and like any weather uncontrollable. You could neither summon it nor dismiss it if it came. When I said "snowed," I could ignore the raw terror and reluctant pride I felt in having a maturing body which, one day, I'd promise to a man. One man only. "Snowed" deferred commitment. In the flurry and rising wind of the storm, "snowed" masked feelings, just as whenever other girls dared speak of sex, they used exaggerated tones of comic and tragic awe to mask what they might really be feeling.

This mixed awe lurked in Melissa Banning's

voice as she let me know that Corbin White had promised to bring to Bear Island the book her mother was reading, *Lady Chatterly's Lover*, written by an Englishman. "Just wait until you read the passages that sizzle," she said Corbin had warned, relishing her power to bring us the forbidden. Hadn't I heard that D. H. Lawrence was as randy as he was common? I didn't know what *randy* meant, and I didn't ask. "He writes about *intercourse*," Melissa said in an impressive whisper.

The deceptive prudery in her voice reminded me of my cousin Nancy Reid, come for a visit in summer from South Carolina, with her salacious tales of blood and barely averted public shame.

"And there I was—Margaret Leigh, there I was, in a convertible—the top down, sun pouring down on us, it was like sliding through town on butter, me in the front seat with this gorgeous *bau-ee*, this divine creature, and right then and there I could feel the blood. It's stained through one Kotex already, it's nearly through the second. He's talking to me about *foot-bawl* and the weekend *paw-tee*—he wants me to wear his class ring on a ribbon around my neck! I can tell he's snowed, he's in a white-out blizzard, and all the while, here's the blood coming! I'm flooding! It's gone through my panties, through the first crinoline—I've got on five crinolines, but it's no good, it's through the next . . . and the next . . . "

She'd been forced to run through her front door, because the blood was just at the last crinoline, brimming toward her skirt. "I just about *died*," she assured me.

I nodded, but I couldn't imagine Armistead Merriweather telling such a story. I couldn't imagine anyone in St. Catherine's Middle School telling it. As if reading my mind, Nancy Reid concluded. "Of course I couldn't tell *muh-ther*. I only told my friends, the closest ones to me at the sleep-over. And only with all the lights turned off."

"I wouldn't know," my mother replied when I asked her what was so awful about *Lady Chatterly's Lover*. Why, no one she knew would read such a book! Airy and too easily dismissive, she forgot to ask me why I was asking. Perhaps she trusted me, or perhaps she had something to hide. And so it was with a little guilt that, on a hunch, I searched her dresser drawers the next afternoon as she walked down to Stanley's Market, and I found the forbidden book. It was giving off heat in her slips and stockings. As I turned the pages, reading quickly, I listened for mother's returning footsteps on the front porch. Lady Chatterly's lover was the game-keeper of her estate, and he lived in a cottage, which she would visit. When they were naked, he touched the two openings between her legs and said, "And I don't mind if ye shits or pisses. I like a woman who can shit and piss." His ruff of pubic hair was red. I read as much as I dared and replaced the book in its hiding place. Then I made a resolve. I would tell her I'd found it, but I wouldn't tell her I'd read any of it. We could both have our lurid little secrets.

"It's not as terrible a book as they say," she told me, after a pause.

"Now don't you tell your friends your mother's reading it!" she exclaimed shortly.

"That man, that man in the book, he really knows what a woman likes," she mused. The smile on her face stunned me. It was tender, as if she had made the man in the book her lover just by reading the book. Mistaking my expression, she added, "Your father's a little rough."

She shouldn't be telling me that, I thought, wishing I hadn't tried to trip her up, catch her in a lie, shock her with my knowing her secret. She possessed, I realized, secrets I couldn't hope to fathom, secrets that tipped into view in the quick lightning flash of words that gave me a glimpse of the woman my mother was, the man my father was. In that flickering light, I'd see but I wouldn't know what I'd seen, and then it would be dark again. Telling me once about her wedding day, she described her dress, the church, Aunt T's house made festive with greens and flowers, the box of baked sweets the cooks sent them off with, the smell of the ocean when she and Dad arrived at Virginia Beach. "We were so happy," she said. Then, "And next morning on the boardwalk I could hardly walk, I was so sore."

She shouldn't be telling me that, I remembered thinking then, too. Mom didn't talk to my sister like this. Mom needed a friend, I realized—and I was it.

Becoming a woman appeared to be a process of repeated shocks and perplexities. I had existed until now in a lull. Until now I had floated in shallow waters. Now the tide was in, bringing with it a stiff undertow, and I was borne by currents I couldn't anticipate or govern. My body had a mind of its own. I could obey Commandments, school regulations, my parents' rules. I could obediently refrain from stealing, I could keep to schedules and codes, I could follow *Proverbs* and not call my sister a fool, I could say "Yes, Sir" when my father's eyes darkened and he could no longer be teased by "Poor Daddy, all alone in a house with three women!" But I couldn't ask my breasts to stop growing. I could tweeze the random hairs that sprouted between my eyebrows, but I couldn't ask the month blood not to stain my bed sheets.

In the summer, I longed for the simplicity of earlier trips to Virginia Beach. In earlier years, I would run on the beach, shoot the waves with Dad, eat a full plate of Mom's rare sirloin and new potatoes, rough house with Elizabeth and her black cocker spaniel who chased fiddler crabs into their sand holes on the beach. Now I worried that my Kotex showed in the crotch of my bathing suit. *Take frequent showers*, counseled the pamphlets on female hygiene, but Mom rationed water, Kotex, shampoo. Now at the beach we dressed up in the afternoons and attended "dances" with the famous Lester Lannin band. Invited to dance, or not, all the wall flowers and short boys joined in a daisy ring of follow-the-leader—the band called it the "bunny hop." *Dah de dah de dah dah, dah de dah. Dah de dah de dah dah. DAH DAH DAH.* The rhythm pounded like surf as we kicked and hopped, holding on to each other's waists. I worried that I smelled like rotting fish. Elizabeth and I refused temptations of salt water taffy and Coca Colas, spending our money on perfume, powder, bobby pins, and deodorant. Mom and Dad had rented a cottage on the cheap because it was owned by a family whose daughter Mom had taught in second grade. The next week we stayed for free at a cottage owned by Elizabeth's friend Cabell's unmarried aunt. "Divorced, I'll bet," grumbled Mom, looking around the cottage as if for a lurking gamekeeper.

On rainy afternoons, Elizabeth and I stayed in the spare bedroom and listened to the aunt's records, Frank Sinatra singing "Autumn Leaves" and other songs of love and loss. Over and over we played them to drown out our laughter and chagrin as we read Cabell's aunt's love letters, which we'd found bundled and shoved behind the records. They had been written by a Navy man, a sailor. "I'm polishing my white shoes buck naked on my bunk. You should see me!" he had written. Our eyes widened to take him in, and we giggled.

"I think he's a bit too coy," Elizabeth suggested, and we exhausted ourselves in a fit of laughter, avoiding what we wouldn't say.

Committed to being virgins, sworn to virtue until we gave ourselves to the "right" man, we couldn't admit that already we touched ourselves in secret, tasting for ourselves a pleasure we weren't supposed to know lay so near at hand. Until you were with a man, it didn't count, it didn't exist. *Since you went away, the days grow longer . . .* sang Sinatra, and the mournful longing in his voice would all but blot out the image of a suitor buck naked but for his own shoe polish, writing letters to the beloved he wanted with him in his bunk.

Thrown together on vacation, Elizabeth and I were without the refuge of separate friends, separate classrooms, separate bedrooms, and we fashioned an alliance of sorts. "I'm ashamed of my fat," she confessed one afternoon as she tried to conceal her body from my view as we changed into our bathing suits. For once I didn't respond with a fact or observation I'd been harboring to squelch her. I didn't say, "Well, if you hadn't gone and eaten the entire cake on the sly . . . ." She had eaten a cake. Just before we left for the beach cousin Sandra, for whose young children Elizabeth had been baby sitting, had called to tell Mom just that. I'd waited to hear Mom reprimand my sister, but instead she'd only confided her embarrassment to me. Perhaps Mom wanted peace. She had in April bribed Elizabeth with an early birthday present, saying "I'll give it to you if you'll only stop nagging me." Now I said nothing to Elizabeth about the case of the disappearing cake. Instead, hearing my sister's candid shame, I felt a thrill of sympathy, surprised to feel it, more surprised to be glad to.

"Mom stuffs us," I agreed. Gone was my contempt for my sister's choice of favorite foods—hot dogs, spaghetti, chicken drumsticks, milky way candy bars, chocolate covered cherries, butterscotch almond ice cream, baloney. Gone was my scorn for her plump thighs and calves, her double chin, the soft and pasty white skin of the bulge her belly made, the dimples in cream look to the flesh over her ribcage. We had a common goal—to be sleek as movie starlets. And we had a common enemy in our mother, who couldn't help herself—or us—but urged on us fried chicken, mashed potatoes with pan gravy and butter, sausages, batter bread, black-eyed peas and stewed tomatoes with sugar; our mother, who in Richmond on summer nights several times a week would call out, "Daddy go and get your three girls double dip ice cream cones." And she'd call out the flavors she wanted for each of us, the chocolate I found hard to resist, her own peaches and cream, and the butterscotch for Elizabeth.

Quietly Elizabeth and I began to help each other hide food, sneaking half of a sandwich beneath the table to the complicit cocker spaniel, wadding toast into a napkin or a pocket, stuffing fist-sized lumps under cushions or into dresser drawers, reminding each other to retrieve them and throw them out before the mayonnaise turned rancid and the bread blued. It was an uneasy alliance. Elizabeth mocked me with dramatic disgust when I'd wiggle a finger down my throat to make myself throw up. And I'd taunt her when she couldn't resist gobbling half a box of salt water taffy or chocolates. But momentary slips and stings were ameliorated by our generally united front: we would be beautiful. Thin and svelte, who could resist us?

Returned to Richmond, Mom and Dad increased our weekly allowances so that we might save for clothes we wanted for school. I'd go to Steve and Anna's to look, then take the bus downtown to Miller & Rhoades, buying whatever came closest to what was fashionable in the West End. With me once in Steve and Anna's, Mom placed a mink cuffed collar, which could also double as a hat, onto my head, stood back, and gazed at me with admiration. It did look nice—but mink? The salesgirl, sensing a sale, closed in with flattery Mom could neither resist nor afford. So that she wouldn't be embarrassed, I adopted a cool and distanced expression, a regal detachment close to boredom. I removed the little crown of mink and flipped it back on its shelf. No, I didn't want it.

And really, where would I wear it? At the dinner table? At the dinner table, nightly the struggles with Mom over calories and serving sizes became a stubborn stand-off which Dad resolved by speaking with his mouth full in a curt voice to demand that we obey our mother. More back-talk, we'd be grounded. Sullenly I picked at my food, then gave up and gulped what I was compelled to eat, hid what I could.

I was, in fact, starving, and in school I ate hungrily. Or I took only one forlorn bite of the sandwich and one more of the apple as Melissa regarded me critically. When I said I was too fat, she shook her head and ate a competitively smaller bite of her own sandwich. If I said I was too thin, automatically repeating my mother's pronouncements, she cast a furtive glance of amusement toward any nearby friend. Too thin! Her gaze settled below my collarbone seven inches. Suddenly I understood. No matter how thin I became, no matter how flat my belly, slim my hips, taut my buttocks, I had breasts. I had big breasts, my mother's breasts: I would look just like her. A stout edifice with an expansive front porch.

At home I began to sequester more food, and now not simply to support the alliance I'd made with my sister. I was angry at my breasts and at my mother, the source of my inheritance, never mind that she once mournfully suggested that I should not only be grateful for the engineering of the modern bra, but grateful to have a mother who would buy the bras I needed. As a girl in the country she'd had no money for a bra, and as her breasts lengthened and spread, she had sewn handkerchiefs together to cover them, using ribbons to hoist them higher. Whereas I had earlier responded with sympathy as she described that not quite credible brassiere, now the story only made me angry. She knew what it felt like to be too big. She had felt a similar awkward shame. She too had walked into study hall with her head high and her shoulders tilted forward and ever so slightly rounded, hoping to conceal her breasts. Uncertainty she would have disguised as dignity as she entered a room with her notebook held before her like a heavy platter, her cheeks unbearably pink. Mrs. Lewis helped Cookie count calories; Mrs. Banning split a turkey sandwich between Melissa and me and gave Melissa, who was dieting, the "smaller half." Why couldn't Mom help me? Why couldn't she see me?

In order to see myself, I locked myself into my sister's bathroom and took off all my clothes. Hers was the only interior door in the house that locked. I stood on my toes to see more of me in the small, high mirror. I preened. I struck a pose. I touched myself here and there and down there. I closed my eyes and imagined a man who would see me. That's all I could manage to say: a man. I had no boyfriend, no one specifically in mind. Outside the bathroom window, a spring robin bumped and pecked at the window glass, pecked and fluttered, flew away, flew back, fluttered and pecked rapidly, madly, repeating the nonsense over and over, seeing himself as a rival male, or as his own mate, I couldn't tell. I laughed at the robin. Silly bird that couldn't see itself.

Before Cotillions in the winter, I'd sit at the vanity table Mom had bought for Elizabeth's room. She had starched the frilly white skirt, rubbed the glass top to a shine that squeaked. Every Southern young lady should have one, she said. Dressed up and wearing the only shade of lipstick Mom allowed— "powder pink"—I studied my face to see what others saw when they looked at me. The lowered lights in the room made the lipstick appear darker than it was. The vanity table sat where my piano had been moved in my last year of piano lessons. Seated now in my finery, I gazed uncertainly at a face and flesh that were, according to the preacher in Ecclesiastes, grass: *Vanity, Vanity—All is Vanity*, said the Preacher.

I went to First Presbyterian now, because a few of my classmates went there. Unbelievably, Mom and Dad had allowed Elizabeth and me to change our memberships, and they attended the church with us, keeping their memberships intact, however, at St. Giles. "We're doing it for the girls," I heard Mom tell Floyd Adams when he phoned, puzzled. To change churches for reasons I secretly considered frivolous was vanity, too. I divided my attention between the service and watching other families. I watched Alan Davis and his family in their accustomed pew. Formerly our neighbors on Lexington Road, the Davis family had moved to Three Chopt Road, a better address, and Alan was the smoothest dancer at Cotillion. Louise Hamilton, an Upper School girl whose family was remarkably wealthy, swept into her pew, always late, heavy gold bracelets clanking against the wooden pews when either she or her mother reached for the hymnal. Mrs. Hamilton wore a full length mink coat. Everything Louise owned was monogrammed—even the door of the turquoise Thunderbird she'd been given for her sixteenth birthday bore her initials. *Better a handful of quietness than two hands full of toil and a striving after wind.* I repeated the words in my mind after the preacher said them. Changing churches made me doubt myself—wasn't this the toil and striving after wind the Preacher berated? And so was this struggle to dress right, dress up, be beautiful.

Before the mirror of the vanity table, I tried to see myself through the eyes of my dance partner, whoever he would be. I tried to see myself as Kent Lewis would see me. As Melissa or Carolyn or Corbin, Armistead Merriweather or Meade Davidson would see me. Only when I saw myself as my mother would see me was I beautiful, and that was embarrassing, because she saw—I had to admit it—herself. "It's all up hill until you're seventeen," she had told me. "And it's downhill after that." Her words were dismaying. I didn't think I was beautiful yet, and I only had a few more years, if she were right, to become beautiful before the gradual decline began. My mother had grayed early, and her breasts had obeyed the laws of gravity, child-bearing, and nursing. She'd told me that "once upon a time" she had been "raahther beautiful" drawing out the "ah" vowel until it was as velvety as her pride.

She had her pride, I had mine, I thought grimly, hitching back a bra strap. At least I hadn't let the girls at the slumber party peer at my breasts. It seemed a long time ago, that slumber party. We'd played strip poker, and I had lost. Cookie, sensing the conspiracy to embarrass us, had thrown in her cards early, complaining that she really didn't understand the game. Too proud for such a claim, which would have been an accurate one, I played hand after hand until I was sitting there in my cup C bra and panties. This is as far as I'll go, I'd protested. You'll just have to imagine the rest, I'd said, smug the following morning when Melissa was teased about her sparse pubic hair, through which we could see a little mosquito bite swelling itchy and perilously, just *there* on the outer rim of the pubic fold. The nerve of that mosquito.

"It's harmless," Mrs. Parrish had remarked to Mom, who had mortified me by calling to complain about the strip poker.

"They're just at that age, curious. I'd rather have them explore the gifts and perils of the flesh together and at home than . . ."

"Don't they have sisters?" Mom finally laughed.

"Only some of them do," said the woman who had married the man Aunt Billie once had dated. "Don't worry. They're a lot more prudish than we are. We raised them right."

I put down the receiver on the other phone quietly, hoping they hadn't heard me listening on the line as if my life, or reputation, depended on it.

"Women Rule the World," Mrs. McCue had decreed in an Upper School assembly a few years before. The upper grades studied above ground in Ellett Hall. Now I sat with other ninth and tenth graders in the basement room of Bacot Hall, called Lower Study Hall. If we studied hard, we would rise to the Upper Study Hall, the upper ranks of the school.

Mrs. McCue had retired, but her words had not. Before us was Miss Abbey Castle, her successor, repeating Mrs. McCue's words as, late to the morning assembly by twenty minutes, I whispered my excuses to Miss West before I prepared to slink to my seat in shame. I'd been in the bathroom, sick, I told her. Actually I'd been in the library reading in the stacks and had lost track of time.

Speaking before the lower grades, Miss Castle, Head of Upper School, was busy preparing us for St. Catherine's Day at the end of the month. On that day, a Senior voted most like St. Catherine would appear before the entire Upper School in McVey Auditorium, dressed and crowned like the Saint the school honored for her faith and for the martyrdom that had elevated her. Miss Castle then repeated Mrs. McCue's famous dictum, affirming the moral preeminence of women in our civilization. Although men might hold the visible positions of power and influence, behind every President, Senator, General, and business executive, there was a woman: his mother. Women ruled because, standing behind, like a good wind at your back, women trained the minds and governed the hearts of those children who became the world's leaders. Wives took over where mothers left off. "You are in training to be the 'unacknowledged legislators of the world,'" Mrs. McCue was said to have concluded proudly, quoting an English poet.

I had seen Mrs. McCue's portrait in Ellett Hall, a trim woman in good shoe leather and a wool suit, her face as Scottish as those I would, years later, see in restored photographs of women on the island of Harris, fulling the wool that would be sewn into Harris tweed jackets, like those later worn by the natty fathers of St. Catherine's girls in Richmond. Miss Castle revived Mrs. McCue's words with a gaiety that proclaimed them gospel. Years later I'd recognize that the gaiety, a mask for defiance and resignation, was intended to offer us comfort as we learned to accept our place in the scheme of things. It also allowed the comforter herself to be comforted. At the time, the boast fell on my ears without any slur of complicity. Hearing, I was simply pleased.

Rigorous in their self-discipline, enthusiastic in their scholarship, their aspirations high, their expectations demanding, many of our teachers were elderly ladies who still wore their fathers' names. Miss West, Miss Castle, Miss McKenney, Miss Fitchett, Miss Walton, Miss Keim, Miss Ruffin, Miss Salley. No one called them old maids. Old Maids was a card game; our teachers were authorities to be reckoned with. The celebrated prank of locking Middle School's Miss Thruston in the lavatory adjacent to her class room would not be tried in Upper School. In my new studies, whole worlds were opening to me, and the heralds of the unlocked doors were these maiden ladies who had missed their chances to stand each behind a man and rule. But they didn't need that opportunity to exercise their wisdom and authority. They had us.

In rare moments of day-dreaming in class, I studied my teachers.

Miss West taught us Latin. Her hair might be too short, her glasses too cat-eyed, her stomach prominent, her breath bad, but she loved the Latin language and Roman civilization so much I forgave her transgressions of appearance. Latin she raised from the dead, tracing our English words to their Latin roots, fulfilling her duty to deliver me spellbound to Miss Fitchett's Julius Caesar, Cicero, and Virgil.

Behind those Roman statesmen in togas stood tiny Miss Fitchett, who embodied her name, swatting away the indecisive as if it were a fly.

Behind the Old Testament stood Miss McKenney.

"What did you girls see when your parents read you about Noah and the Ark," she challenged. I remembered imagining a globe of water, an atlas of flooded plains, a tub-like boat rocking on the waves of the South Pole. When no one said anything, I offered these images, and Miss McKenney smiled. "Good, that's good. Your parents taught you to believe *literally* every word." She paused. "You saw doves and rainbows, too, I suppose." We nodded. I watched the corn-gold stubble over her upper lip, a mustache brilliant in the sidelong sunlight coming in the classroom window. "But that was seeing through a glass darkly." Again she paused. "Now you must learn the spirit of the old stories. You must learn to see by *metaphor*," and she began to rework the story. I gasped. We had permission to think for ourselves, even about *The Bible*?

Miss Ruthalia Keim, our French teacher, was given to humming Maurice Chevalier as she made a quick turn on tiny ankles, finishing with a wiggle of her ample body. Her bobbed gray hair and bangs fringed an equine face. Down she'd plop, elbows on the low teacher's desk, standing with her generous rear end jutted out, facing the class with her low neckline and elderly cleavage. From this position, smiling knowingly, she'd quiz us on vocabulary, tossing out whole sentences of complex French to us. We had to be daring enough to return aloud a reply in French. "Je ne sais pas," was heresy.

Mrs. Coleman, my only married teacher, taught as sweetly as a grandmother would, gaining her authority through a humility so evident that she became transparent. Reading aloud passages from Dickens or Shakespeare, she vanished, and in her place stood Sidney Carton. Pip. Puck. Lady Macbeth. Through her we met Silas Marner. Jane Eyre. Becky Sharpe.

"You really like reading books, don't you," Melissa said, close on my elbow as we left Mrs. Coleman's classroom. "I mean, you really *do*, don't you?"

She's right, I thought, amazed that her simple, succinct sentence summed me up. I couldn't have said it myself, even though I knew that in the hours I spent reading, I never missed a living human soul. Unwittingly, Melissa Banning had handed me myself. A lover of books. That was who I was. That was me.

"You're what my mother calls a *blue stocking*," she added, but the label—perhaps intended to link me to the fate of an old maid—fluttered away. I knew Melissa well enough by now to recognize her talent for giving a compliment and mocking it with a little sting.

"You're right," I said, disarming the sting with a smile.

Spending more time at her house now than at Cookie Lewis', I considered Melissa my best friend in the large group of girls that regularly met on Saturdays to play bridge, four tables of us. We had organized the bridge club as our mothers organized theirs—so I was told. In any attempt to emulate our social mothers, I was at a disadvantage. My parents, I realized, had no social life beyond what they'd known at St. Giles, from which they were now distanced. I wondered if they missed their previous participation in choir practice and deacon's meetings, covered dish suppers and study groups. The thought of their increasing isolation glanced by me and fluttered off. I was focused on my own social life, even though when it came time to organize the bridge club meetings, I stood back and let the other girls make the arrangements. The location of our meetings rotated, and the hostess of the day served a lunch of sandwiches, chips, cupcakes, and coca-colas. Corbin White brought her older sister's cigarettes, or if we were in Melissa's paneled basement, finding packs of cigarettes behind the bar was a snap. She had older brothers, and both of her parents smoked.

I learned the game of bridge quickly, taking out books from the library and devouring Charles Goren's column in the newspaper. I loved the sly innuendo of bidding, the discipline of counting cards, the triumph of the trump. A giddy pleasure it was to figure out who held the Jack, who the King, reserving my Queen to cancel the Jack when the unsuspecting opposition played it, protecting her from the King, should that more powerful card be lurking. All of us, the "smart" girls, strove for the ideal bridge table—a game played with savvy and acumen, with no table talk or distractions.

Elizabeth mocked us. It was school on Saturday, she said. Had I made an "A" in bridge yet?

So different from my family, the Bannings fascinated me with their worldliness. Mr. and Mrs. Banning were socially engaged every Saturday night. They went to the Country Club, to the Commonwealth Club, to the houses of their friends for drinks and dinner. They also dressed up, black tie and evening gown. Mrs. Banning descended the basement stairs one evening, ostensibly to remind Melissa and me of a minor duty, actually to display her purple satin dress with a daring single shoulder strap.

I gasped, "You look beautiful!"

Mrs. Banning smiled grandly.

Making a face, Melissa turned away from her mother. The spitting image of her plain father, she did not choose to compliment her mother, who worked hard to remain beautiful. Whenever her mother ate an entire box of Sara Lee cupcakes, Melissa told me, she would perform rigorous exercises—in the nude— in the privacy of her bedroom. Perhaps she wanted to see her indiscretions melting away. We had all seen Mrs. Banning striding up and down Grove Avenue's sidewalks grimly, too absorbed to acknowledge the toots of the horn a friend might sound to encourage her onward. Her curious incivility fascinated me, and I gradually realized that Mrs. Banning wanted to be ignored. She was merely "out for a walk." She wasn't "exercising." A lady was effortlessly fit and trim or effortlessly pleasing and plump. Willing herself thin, Mrs. Banning resembled the grim, angry reaper. She also resembled my mother when she was angry at my refusals to eat, frustrated by her failure to persuade or force down me another mouthful. To be thin, my plump mother asserted, was *unnatural*.

One Saturday evening when Melissa's parents were due to go out for the evening, her brother Henry Banning was hosting a party for his friends, home for the semester. College age, they seemed as remote as Rock Hudson, although not as handsome.

"You girls stay upstairs, let the boys have the basement to themselves," Mrs. Banning advised as she gathered her gloves and checked her lipstick in the hall mirror. Mr. Banning nodded, tossing a scribbled phone number on the hall table. He seemed impatient.

My father had recently gone to Ted Banning's office to sell him tickets for a church raffle. Too hurried to hear out my father's carefully rehearsed words, he'd tossed the required money on the desk. "Sure, sure," he said, looking at his watch. My father, who had grown up with Ted Banning, was incensed. I could imagine him pausing, jaw slack, eyes darkening—insulted. "Don't offer money if you don't really want to go," Dad had told him. I knew the tone of voice he'd have used. Hoarse, shocked, a touch prudish.

"C'mon, Margaret," Mr. Banning said, and my shoulders twitched, as if he might have been reading my mind. But he was only getting after his wife, whose name was also Margaret.

From Melissa's bedroom upstairs, we heard the music of the Kingston Trio and laughter. A male voice called up the stairs, something about "robbing the cradle." Ill at ease, Melissa kept opening her door and peering over the banister whenever she heard the front door bell. Her brother had promised a modest gathering, subdued and chummy—cards, drinks, a few girls back from college, old pals. Considered something of a disappointment to his ambitious parents, Henry Banning squired about with his wealthy friends, all with reputations for careless banter and the allure of dissolution. Some of these boys had been at Horace Montfort's house the night it burned to the ground in the early hours of the morning. Had a cigarette been dropped in between sofa cushions? No one knew for sure. Horace's young brother had not made it out of the burning house, and so Henry Banning and his cronies had about them the glamour of deadly danger and unpunished guilt.

Melissa and I were playing double solitaire in her room when a knock on the door became a door rapidly opened and closed behind a flustered young woman. "Do you have a phone up here," she cried, "I have to use the telephone immediately!"

She was blonde, dressed in good wool, a gold charm bracelet. Her eyes sought ours for comfort or rescue—and remained aloof. We were, she was discovering, so much younger than she. Melissa gave her the phone, and the girl asked if she could be alone in the room when she used it. To my surprise, Melissa said no.

Turning her back to us, the girl began talking rapidly, asking for a ride home. Yes, right away. No, she couldn't call a cab. She wanted to be picked up as soon as possible. She'd say why later. No, she couldn't tell him now.

Handing the phone receiver back to Melissa, the girl asked if she might stay upstairs until her ride arrived. We made attempts at conversation, but she was too nervous to sustain sentences. I remember that she attended Wellesley College. When the front door bell rang, she leapt up, dashed down the stairs, leaving behind the scent of her perfume, the door closing on the abrupt voice of whoever it was had come to bear her away.

What was it all about?

"I'll bet nothing much," Melissa declared. "She seemed awfully naïve to me."

"She was scared," I suggested.

"You don't have brothers," Melissa said, sounding

as worldly as her mother. "I'll bet Goldilocks doesn't either." Then she marched downstairs to talk to her brother. She was chuckling when she returned.

"Not to worry," she told me. "There was a little teasing and Cinderella in distress didn't take it well."

"What did they say?"

"Oh, you know . . . boys. There was a teddy bear downstairs and somebody opened its legs and patted it. No big deal. *May I pat you on the po-po?* Henry Banning asked the girl, and he demonstrated what he wanted to do, with the bear."

"Who was she?"

"A friend of a friend. Girl from out of town, a blind date. I'll bet her friend's dad was put out to have to come pick her up."

I frowned. "What if it had been you or me. Wouldn't your . . ." and I stopped. No, I wouldn't have found it easy to call Mr. Banning for a ride home, had I been the Cinderella with the po-po a rich boy wanted to pat. But how odd, I thought, how odd that Melissa was responding this way. Of all our friends, she was the one most interested in social infractions. Who was making out on a date? How far did she go? She talked about "getting to first base" or second or third, and "going all the way." You can kiss, but don't tell Melissa was the way one friend put it. We all knew the probable fate of any girl foolish enough to go "all the way." Pregnancy, personal disgrace, family humiliation—it started innocently enough, with a kiss; but that kiss was a flirtation with the devil.

"It was just talk," Melissa insisted. "No one did anything."

"Don't be such a Pollyanna," she said next, more sharply. Then she laughed. "That girl just could have used a little more gumption."

"Women rule the world," I rejoined, glad for a platitude that would cover my confusion.

Had I told my mother about the distressed college girl, she would perhaps have offered familiar advice: the girl needed to have more faith. If you had faith, you could do anything. With faith, any trial might be endured. If you had faith, you had only to wait a moment and God's grace would deliver you. With faith, you could renounce any temptation, sure of success; overcome any loss, certain of restoration. Whenever I listened to my mother echo the words of assurance given from the pulpit, I would shake my head. It sounded too easy. *Only have faith.* Faith and, well . . . a little gumption and character.

At fifteen, my character had largely been untested. Mrs. Coleman, citing Milton, said that our virtues were "cloistered," and that was just fine, she smiled. We were heroines in training.

Like everyone else, she seemed to think that a girl's virtue and her virginity were one and the same. If that were true, certainly I could agree that I had not yet been tested and hardly tempted. My "beaux," as my mother liked to refer to them, hadn't been dangerously appealing. Donald Smith had kissed me before a Cotillion, hastily, as if unsure of the sweetness of his breath, or—worse thought—of mine. Lowndes Nelson had phoned to ask me over to Garland Moore's house in the afternoon. They had planned a little music and dancing. Other girls would be there, he said. They were "nice" boys, and so I had bicycled over. Other girls were there; Garland's mother was not. Innocent enough, I thought, and enough *not* that it was interesting. I stayed and tried to do the new dance steps—the chicken, the mashed potato, the tried and true jitterbug. Moving toward each other for a slower dance, Lowndes and I were both startled when his hard penis—it had to be that—pushed into my skirt, grazing my pubis. I felt him, he felt me, and we leapt apart as if lightning had struck the floor between us. The shock of contact had been too intimate and, unprepared for it, we looked away, pretending nothing had happened, then danced, careful to keep our bodies far apart.

More recently John Page Williams, the son of a minister with a name my mother ranked "as old as Virginia," was escorting me to the movies every other weekend. We weren't "snowed." John Page was licensed to drive, and when we single dated, he would count "pididdles"—cars on the highway with only one headlight on. When he saw a "pididdle," he said I owed him a kiss. "Who made that rule?" I laughed, but when he parked the car in front of my house—with the front porch light on, bright as stage lighting and meant to discourage the devil's temptations, I let him kiss me.

Melissa would write in my yearbook at the year's close, "Be good with J.P." She might have saved her ink. The temptations offered by Satan, said to be a smooth talker, had left me cold. I was content to wait and see who would enter my life and change it. Wasn't that the plot line?

Waiting, I fixed my eyes on the handsome tenor in the First Presbyterian Church choir, concocting romantic encounters. Not as handsome as Cary Grant or William Holden, nor as polished and misunderstood as Mr. Darcy in *Pride and Prejudice*, nor as doomed as Sydney Carton in *A Tale of Two Cities*, nor as wealthy and decadent as many a European in Henry James, he was—the handsome chorister—at least as distant and more malleable. I thought up what he would say to me and what I would reply. I let his words—my words—swell and roll in my head, where I could be as passionate as I dared, as demure as called for.

It would have been far more daring to summon into my fantasies the boys I danced with, or yearned to dance with, at the boy-girl weekend parties I was occasionally invited to attend. With parents upstairs, teenagers gathered in the recreation room of the basement or in the den, with fast music followed by slow music followed by fast music, the lights lowered or turned back on by the chaperoning parent. These parties netted me at best a waltz with tall Seldon Harris or Benjy Winn, during which I had to be careful not to dance too close because the other wall flowers, from whose tight bouquet I was only temporarily released, were watching to see *if* flesh pressed, *where* it pressed, and *how long*.

Once, just once, Seldon's fingers brushed my

shoulder carelessly, grazing near my collarbone, or lower, and I felt between my legs a stupendous flash of yearning. It was sudden, unbidden.

"Sexual intercourse is a communion," as my mother described it. It was sacred. It was like the Lord's Supper. Partaken. Holy. Sanctioned only by married love and sacrifice. I wondered if Mom wanted us plump and unattractive so that the boys would stay away. It would be easier then to keep her daughters virginal. Whether I believed these thoughts or not, fat felt like punishment.

I wondered if the many lovers in the movies were punished because their attitudes toward lovemaking were not so devout. In wedlock or out of it, women who were too ambitious or too successful— like Eleanor Parker in *Interrupted Melody*—suffered. At the height of her operatic career and married to a good man, Glen Ford, partaking of life's abundance, she was struck down with polio. Or Jane Wyman, struck blind and having to have her sight restored in a risky operation performed by the man she'd wrongly spurned, Rock Hudson. Or Deborah Kerr, struck by a car as she was running to her tryst with Cary Grant, whom love had reformed from roue to responsible fiancee. They would both have to suffer before they could have each other. In the movies, the suffering gave new meaning to romance. No passion was legitimate without it.

Into a darkened and candlelit McVey auditorium, the Upper School filed quietly, each class sitting together as a class, waiting for the curtain to be raised on the senior most like St. Catherine. She had been broken on the wheel in Egypt, in Alexandria. The seniors' gold school rings, designed to resemble rings with family crests engraved on them, showed the Crown of Victory and the Wheel of Pain that were the proof of her faith and love. The voting for the girl who would be St. Catherine had been very close, so said the rumors, and there was a sense of suspense. Who would she be?

The curtain rumpled, rippled, then tugged itself into an ogee arch that made an alcove of light. I recognized the Standard Bearer, kneeling before St. Catherine's, dressed in choir robes. She represented our devotion to the martyred saint. I did not, however, recognize St. Catherine, perhaps because of her crown or the make-up, or more likely because she was a boarding student. There was whispering among a few of the seniors. They clearly knew who she was—a girl like them who took Latin or French, who dissected frogs, who played hockey or tennis, and who beyond any worldly accomplishment was well known for acts of tender self-abnegation, doing what was needful, never for her own sake, but for God's.

I liked not knowing who she was. Now I could see the St. Catherine before me, dressed in her long silk dress and crown of fulfillment, as the Saint herself, or at least as close as wardrobe and make-up allowed in the transformation of an ordinary mortal who had, in all probability, kissed boys. If you believed the back lighting, the saint was shot through with light from the far side of the world's limits. Before the upright, slender, and awkwardly transfigured image of the martyr, before this living icon that had opened up to an inner dimension with clarity and humility, I felt fallen. I was a sprawl of darkness and division. I was the heart's perplexity incarnate. I pressed further back into my seat in the dark auditorium as the Glee Club and assembled classes began singing "Jerusalem." It was a very strange moment, this one, with St. Catherine radiantly before me—whole, virginal, and inexplicable.

John Pineda

Excerpt from *Sleep in Me*

Learning the Language

Because we were boys, not yet teenagers, we would laugh to ourselves when we said words like fuck or cocksucker or cunt. We would gather what little bit of money we could find around our houses, usually in the sticky folds of couches, and walk up to the gas station on Battlefield Boulevard. People filling their cars before heading further into Great Bridge would stare at us like we were strays. You could tell by their pursed lips. They were hoping we wouldn't wander any farther than where we were. Our hair tousled, our shirts stretched, brushed with grass stains and some blood garnered from a neighborhood football game. Each of us was a pariah in-training.

Sometimes, emboldened, we'd stare back in disgust or yell things and flip them off. It was all part of the role. They expected it of us. At the pay counter, we'd smirk at the receding hairline of the clerk, an old speckled man with palsy who would rather read his paper than have to look his customers in the eye. We blessed this apathy. Word had gotten around, too. His inattention couldn't have been better. While towers of coins tumbled into his shaky hand, we'd demand soft packs of Marlboro or Camel or Kool brand cigarettes. Without so much as glancing at us, he'd smile.

Sometimes we only wanted the finger-sized, cherry-flavored cigars with crimped tips, the ones kept arranged in a container near the register. They would be next to the single roses wrapped in plastic tubes, vials of green water cupping the clipped stems. In triumph we bore our stash back to the fort, a rusted maintenance van that had been left to rot in a side lot near Timmy's house. Even in warm months, we'd sit inside this van. The doors and windows would be sealed shut, and we'd thumb slowly through issues of *Penthouse* or *Hustler* someone's uncle had given us.

I remember in one there was a woman whose body had been decorated to resemble a landscape. Tiny orange diamond-shaped construction signs balanced on her nipples while Matchbox cars of all sizes lined up in a traffic jam between her breasts. Other cars heading south on the makeshift road of her belly actually disappeared inside her. In another issue, some of the pages would be torn. More often than not there would be a worn oval section between a woman's legs. Of course, we knew what from, and on subsequent pages, there were places where the heads of these naked women should be but weren't. The images beyond violated, but we didn't care. We didn't really think of them as being violated, didn't know the various forms violations could take.

Instead, we'd cough and laugh as we spoke in what we thought was the language of men. We were learning the language. We wanted to become men so badly we'd do whatever we thought was necessary. Break all the rules, if that's what it took. It didn't matter that we had kissed girls already. Or had felt a few up. Everyone had. The van became a sanctum where any knowledge gleaned from the adult world was shared with all. In a full sweat, we'd throw out questions to each other, ask if any of us knew what certain girls from our school would really do. One of us would inevitably offer a story about so and so doing this and that with so and so. I would listen intently, as would the others.

Once, someone put two fingers in the air, the fingers close together like their knuckles were knees to a pair of modest legs. He said, You want to smell what it smells like?

We were nervous, said Fuck, no, but then each took a turn.

Who is it? I said, stepping back, feeling like I had to sneeze.

You don't know? he said, laughing.

Who is it? I said.

Man, it's just your sister, he said.

Of course, I knew it wasn't, but I charged at him anyway. You had to do that. It's what boys did. We fell to the floor, and he was laughing, saying he was just kidding, just kidding for fuck's sake. Soon, all of us were laughing. It was how it was. We were mostly friends, easily forgiven for whatever lines we crossed with one another.

Sorry, he said. I didn't mean your sister.

He brushed dust from his shirt as he stood up. He smiled.It was the kind when people only barely show you their teeth. Gums with just a trace of teeth. Like they have something in their mouth they don't want to let out just yet.

Don't say it, I said. I knew what was coming.

What? he said. Like your mom cares if I tell you.

That's it, I said, and we were down on the floor of the van again.

Beneath the Surface

Before my sister Rica's accident, I thought I might stay a boy forever. If I wasn't roasting inside that abandoned van, scheming under sheets of smoke, I was spending days after school roaming with other boys from the neighborhood. Boys whose names when I think of them now are only ghosts in a far off landscape—Heath, Timothy, Glen. There was even one whose last name was Hill.

Along the rear of Hill's house ran a creek where a part of the land ended and formed a small promise of open water. There we would not hesitate to shoot at the heads of cottonmouths. We'd use .22s instead of Hill's father's 12 or 20-gauge shotguns. We thought we were being responsible by forgoing the larger guns, especially since our antics were done usually from the safety of the dock nearby.

The dock's crinoline tin roof would also shield us from the sun casting long jagged-edged shadows. If we thought about it, we could picture someone holding a giant handsaw above us, a hint of some invisible but imminent danger. If we weren't shooting at something, we were oddly pensive. We'd cast lines through the clouded water and wait for the first bite from anything. *Fish, snake, snapping turtle.* It didn't matter. We wished only for what lived beneath the surface.

One day, on our way down to the creek, we stopped first for ammunition. We crouched in front of Hill's house, where the edge of pavement seemed to unravel at the end of Snowberry Lane. Above us, ragged squirrels were nervous in the clustered oaks and maples. They jumped from branch to branch and scurried spirals up and down the wrinkled trunks.

These trees marked the beginning of a haze every boy in the neighborhood disappeared within. Huddled, like cavemen around a ring of stones nursing a fire through their whispering, we pulled at each black chunk of tarmac still sticky and giving off a blunt sucking sound. Pieces wrenched free were the size of huge brownies, slowly folding in our hands from the heat. In water, they hardened into caustic polygons. They became the primitive tools we lugged in buckets down to the creek.

Low tide was that odd time of day when the murkiness receded and left gray moss-covered banks dimpled with mud and the random blemish of a coiled snake. After the water had seemingly drained into the scattered pools, we would gather up our buckets and head in the direction of uncharted marsh. In our other hands were the enormous pieces of pavement. We'd sling them into puddles and wait for the bait.

The force of each impact would thrust silvered

minnows onto the banks to flail, and we'd walk around them, examining them as they bounced and spun like a handful of BBs released onto a tiled floor. We'd miss some entirely. Others we'd momentarily hold only to have them glide through our fingers. Sometimes we'd end up clutching mud, groping some, and then lucky, we'd slip the bodies into the buckets where we kept a little water for the other minnows. It wasn't much water, just enough to keep them alive.

Later we'd return to the dock with our catch and wait for high tide. With high tide came the monstrous catfish, those bloated and slimy submarines, whiskered and nearly blind. They looked to us to be from another planet. Being boys hinged to this small space of earth, we wanted to do our part. We craved to torture them in the grass.

Then we did.

The Clothespin

It was the year the house always smelled like cabbage. She had read about it, or she knew a girl from school who had tried it and now swore by it. There was always a pair of jeans that needed to be fit into. That, or a bikini. The cabbage would be the answer, the salvation.

It involved filling the deep black pot we normally used to steam crabs, bushels our mother would bring back from roadside stands in North Carolina that we'd redden with Old Bay and boiling water. The cabbage came from nearby farms, too, I think. Rippled heads dropped into the dark gurgling water, softening. They released the ill fragrance of my sister's desire to be thin. It's sad to think about now, but I know it consumed her.

Tinah, my oldest sister, was less affected by this craving to fit in. I don't want to say it was easier for her, because I'm sure it wasn't. At least, not on the surface. With light brown hair and blue eyes, she was a product of our mother's first marriage and looked more like our first cousins at family gatherings in North Carolina than Rica and I ever would. It is no surprise to anyone in our family that Tinah was our father's favorite. She was *Ate,* the oldest daughter, and our father insisted we treat her with the respect Filipino families afforded the eldest. Perhaps a portion of Rica's obsession to be thin and glamorous had to do with her being *mestiza,* part-Filipino. Already an obvious outsider in a community where at that time you were either white or black or some close version of the two. If you were mixed, though, people loved to ask you where you were from. When you said, *Here,* they would shake their head as if saying, Don't be silly, you know what I mean. And when you'd finally answer, *My father is from the Philippines,* they would smile knowingly and nod, as if saying, See, that wasn't so hard now, was it?

Issues of *Cosmo* lay dog-eared and wrinkled on Rica's bed. They were opened to articles on how to look sexy, things to do to drive a guy wild. Pictures of models were circled with markers. I remember Christie Brinkley had endless black spirals around her. Before this magazine, there was *Seventeen* and there were *Tiger Beat* pullout posters of Leif Garrett or John Travolta taped to the back of her bedroom door. I remember Tinah was going to marry Parker Stevenson and Rica was going to marry Shaun Cassidy. Or maybe it was the other way around.

At nights, I would walk into the bathroom and find Rica staring at herself in the mirror. She might be plucking at an obstinate eyebrow or filing her nails, which she kept long and polished and immaculate. Inevitably, she would complain to her reflection, usually about her hair, which she thought was more like horsehair, coarse and thick and black and unruly. In many ways, she was the quintessential teenage American girl—a lingering aversion for most versions of the way she looked. Rarely was she satisfied with her figure, though I always saw her as athletic and lithe.

Most brothers have lots of dirt on their older sisters. That is, if they have older sisters. It is one of the natural laws of this world. I remember coming home one evening after a long game of neighborhood football, my face still tingling from the cool night air, from running headlong into a shadow of bodies that dispersed into boys and voices. My sense of smell was especially acute.

I could smell the sweet, itchy cool scent of freshly mown grass, the shredded stalks of milkweed that marked the unkempt regions of property lines. When I walked into our house, I felt faint from the noxious fumes coming from the kitchen.

The house smelled like piss. Like boiled vinegar and piss. You could stand at the front door and feel the laced steam against your face. I cupped my mouth and forced my way into the kitchen where I found Rica stirring near the steamy cauldron.

She looked more like a witch at that moment than my sister. I almost yelled out but coughed instead. When she turned around to face me, I saw her black mess of hair was held back with a headband. I froze. On her nose was a clothespin. At first I thought she had worn the clothespin because the fumes were too much. This thought struck me, but I laughed anyway. Only afterwards, when she had settled down with a bowl of this broth, did I notice she didn't take off the clothespin. It stayed on. It wasn't for the cabbage at all. It was for her nose. She thought the pinching would straighten it, make it less flat. She thought, if she tried, she could become someone else entirely.

An Endless Retelling

Friends and family had packed our home to celebrate. Our mother had spent the night before getting things ready. Lots of cooking, lots of rearranging one covered casserole dish after the next onto the bowing shelves of our green refrigerator. In each dish were lined rows of lumpia, Filipino eggrolls, and in the deeper ones pancit and chicken adobo. There was also a pot of collard greens seasoned with salted ham, a huge bowl of mustard-based potato salad covered with a crinkled sheet of aluminum foil. In the oven rested a pan of homemade buttermilk biscuits. Some of these dishes had to be reheated, but it didn't matter. There was so much food. Too much.

Even so, our mother kept cooking, busying herself as she prepared fresh meals and set plates of steamy noodles mixed with soy sauce and cooked garlic slices, bowls of fried rice on the nicked wooden table that had to be widened with a leaf in the center. Raised on a farm in North Carolina, our mother knew how to cook Southern, but she had also learned to prepare Filipino dishes from the wives she had met and befriended living on naval bases along the East Coast. With no air conditioning in the house, fans ticked in corners, clicking at intervals to push the warm air around from one person to the next. When the heat gathered around us, we waved it away like it was an incessant fly. Everywhere was the smell of garlic, in the air and in each conversation.

While our mother moved about the kitchen, laughing at whatever anyone said, our father sat in the living room with his hands on his knees. At this point, our parents had been separated for nearly two years, but for reasons still unknown to me, they had not yet divorced. I remember my father kept his suit coat on for his entire stay that night, or at least, whenever I would walk in to see how he was doing, I found him bundled and sitting on the edge of one of the recliners. He looked ready to run off at any moment.

Boo, he said. Go get your sister.

Which one? I said. I hadn't seen Tinah yet and suspected she was off with her boyfriend Eddie delaying her arrival. This was her graduation party, after all. She would show at some point. I could hear our mother's voice above the others in the kitchen. Though he was smiling, my father looked annoyed.

Go get Rica, my father said and gestured to the other room with arched eyebrows and a jolt of the neck. I had seen other Filipinos motion with their lips, but my father never seemed to fully embrace this style of gesturing. His seemed more a functional hybridization, a subtlety better suited to his more serious nature.

Ellen, Rica's friend, had graduated that night as well and was there in our kitchen. She was still wearing her white graduation gown, which had a silver sheen to it from the way the light played against the warbling fabric. Like my sister Rica, Ellen was a pretty girl with a big smile and feathered dark auburn hair. I didn't know if it was her natural color, but if she shared Rica's obsession for makeup and glamour, Ellen's hair color was probably due to an overzealous application of lemon juice and promptly laying out hours afterwards.

I found Rica smiling with her arm around Ellen. Anyone could see that these girls were friends. Our mother, with her apron still tied around the dress she had worn to the ceremony, was snapping a picture of the two of them. In lime green slacks and a yellow Izod shirt, my friend John has his back to them, him leaning across the platters of food to reach the mound of lumpia. This photograph now rests behind a brittle sheet of plastic, in an album that moves surreptitiously throughout the various rooms of our mother's house. As if buoyant the book of photographs will resurface for one of us to thumb through at our family gatherings now. It is the last picture we have of Rica before the accident. I think it is also the last picture of Ellen as well.

I walked back into the living room, and my father just looked at me like I was supposed to hand him something. I know all night he hasn't made his way into the kitchen, which makes me wonder if I should ask if he's hungry. But I don't. I just stand there, as if blocking him from my mother's view, and him from hers. It is the role I have learned to play, to be the go-between in their continual drama.

What's your sister doing? he says.

Taking pictures, I say.

Tell her to come here, he says. You tell her I want to talk to her.

In our family history, there are two stories

about the ensuing conversation that night between Rica and my father. Both have survived in their endless retelling. In my father's version, all he knows is that he doesn't want her to go to Nags Head. He has a bad feeling about all of it. He knows the other high school kids are renting cottages and going down to the beach for the week, and he knows they will be partying and that there will be alcohol. He doesn't want his youngest daughter in the middle of it.

This is your sister Tinah's year, he tells her. *Next year, you can go.*

He knows our mother has already agreed to let her go with her friend Ellen. Because our father no longer lives in this house, he finds his authority has been lessened by his absence. He knows after tonight Rica will get to go no matter what he says, but even knowing this, he makes one last attempt. He offers to give her five hundred dollars to go shopping with so long as she doesn't leave for North Carolina. Rica pauses, smiles. She loves shopping for clothes. He knows this.

In my mother's version, who claims Rica told her this, Rica goes in search of our father and finds him the same as I have, uneasy and out of place in the house he had helped build for this family. Rica hugs him and says, I want you to know that I *know* you love me. The insinuation, of course, is that he didn't show her, that she is the one showing him now. I don't know how much of this is our mother's revision and how much of it is what really happened. Either way, both versions end with our father speechless, without a voice.

My Father, In Some Small Corner of Memory

I don't remember if I called him. Maybe he just happened to be calling the house at the time. I know he was in Bayonne, where he had been living and working in New Jersey. I remember, too, the local news stations were airing reports about four students from Great Bridge involved in a fatal car crash down in the Outer Banks. On TV, one reporter decided to stand next to the cloth-covered wreckage. I saw large maroon blots on the canvas tarp. I wondered why they would feel it necessary to show my sister's blood to the world.

When I heard my father's voice, I immediately said, Dad, but then my heart sank.

Boo, what's going on? he said. His voice was nervous, shaky, like he already knew something bad had happened.

Rica was in a bad accident, I said. A car accident. I could barely speak. My voice felt thin, like a piece of crumpled paper that kept needing to be smoothed. Or a wafer dissolving on the tongue. I could feel it all disappearing, my voice especially, but not before I told him her head had been hurt, that it had *opened some.*

This last part made him cry.

I started crying, too, because I had made my father cry. I was a boy who had made his father cry. I didn't know the exact details of Rica's injury. I was simply the bearer of the burden my father could now begin to carry himself. I knew a dump truck filled with sand had crushed the small Datsun my sister had ridden inside. The dump truck had actually vaulted halfway over the car and halted, grinding the car down before eventually stopping altogether. Lots of her classmates were there to witness the accident.

We would learn later how, because of the impact and the coiling and fusing of these vehicles, it would take rescue workers nearly 35 minutes to jack up the truck so the medics could reach those trapped inside. I remember hearing my father cry and feeling as though I had done something wrong by telling him all that I knew. I should not have said the thing about her head opening.

My father who is always so serious in my memories of him, in this one he's weeping into the phone from hours away. I hold the receiver. I hold it to my ear and say, listening close, *Dad, I know,* but I don't know. There is so much I will never know, and my father, in some small corner of memory, continues

on with his weeping, and it is not for me, his oldest
son, to stop him.

Diorama

You take a shoebox and line the inside with
black construction paper, gluing the back of each
small sheet and pressing it until you feel the clumps
begin to seep. You make angled cuts into folded
squares of aluminum foil. Almost like you're making snowflakes. There is uniformity in the stars you
hang with the clear fishing line.

Behind the ruffled green paper segments taped
to one another and then to the front edge of the
shoebox, you place the magazine cutout of Christie
Brinkley face down. The typed words on the page
opposite the image will resemble the engraved headstones you've seen flush with the ground in various
graveyards. You have stopped playing with G.I. Joes,
but you take one out of the toy box in your brothers'
room, which is the room you share with them, and
place the soldier on top of these words which are really just a woman underneath. When you're done,
you go back into her room and you set the diorama
to the side and get down on your knees and tell God
that all you want is for her to live and not die. That's
all you and everyone else wants. Then you make the
Sign of the Cross out of habit.

You have already heard the way it happened,
the way it might have happened, but here is how it
happened, or at least, how you now think it happened. No one will tell you she folded herself around
the boy in the backseat. She didn't mean to, but the
truck had hit them with such force that the impact
threw her body into the air, and so she thought it
best to give in to the momentum, if she thought
anything at all. The two of them spun and wrapped
further around one another, like a pair of twins in
utero, and before the rescue workers could pry the
dump truck from the car, those standing nearby
could already see the dark red wet on the road. In

each place it landed on the pavement, it spread its tiny fingers wide as if to reach.

When they finally pulled her from the car, she was wearing nothing except a T-shirt of blood. And they had to pry her hands away from her broken face. An impulse for vanity or otherwise, it didn't matter now. It saved her to some degree. On her face they found the dumb expression of one not only knocked unconscious, her mouth open and her eyes dipped back, but also of one ecstatic, like Saint Theresa, her body looking ravaged completely by the Spirit.

Those nearby would not look at her legs now and think of her legs around them, around their waists pulling them to her and pushing away and then pulling, back and forth, the blood this thing between them. They would not see the others and think of them as friends they had partied with the night before, the celebrations still fizzing around in the core of each stunned brain. Instead, they would later repeat the rumor one had ridden a few cars back and just before the accident traded into the car that would not see the dump truck until it was too late.

Or not that way at all, but this way: where there is always distance to cross. In her room, back in Chesapeake, is a green and gold megaphone with the bubbly letters of her cursive on a small sheet of paper taped near the worn metal handle. On the paper are the words in blue ink to cheers she should know, but keeps them there to remind her. She has said these words and released them into Friday nights, under the lights of football stadiums, the words becoming clouds. That same mouth, that smile. Within it the voice that would bore into the vortex of our longing. That voice would be loudest in silence, just before the endless chorus of *Oh Shit!* or *Fuck it!* or *Fuck me!* or *Oh, my God!* or *Please God!* or just *God!* and then the crushing growl of the truck's grill as it pokes its muzzle into where they are.

*   *   *

Or not that way either, but this way, yes, this way: someone on the beach seeing in the distance helicopters descend beyond the bending fence of sea oats, where the beach is no longer real, was never real. And the helicopters then vanish, become the period at the end of this sentence.

Lucinda Roy

Excerpt from *No Right to Remain Silent*

You have the right to remain silent. Anything you say can and will be used against you. . . .

—From the Miranda warning, mandated by the United States Supreme Court (*Miranda v. Arizona*), 1966

April

There is a terrible moment in *The Collector of Treasures*, a volume of stories by the late Bessie Head, a biracial South African writer. The story is called "The Wind and a Boy." In it, Head writes of a grandmother called Sejosenye who is devastated when she learns of the death of her grandchild, Friedman. Friedman is the pride of Sejosenye's life, her reason for living. A policeman delivers the news of Friedman's death to her: the boy has been knocked off his bicycle by a truck and run over. It is the only time the policeman appears in the story. It is the grandmother's agonized response to the news that has always haunted me. "Can't you return those words back?" she asks him, as if death has no more permanence than an item purchased in a store. Her simple question reverberates with pain. The policeman—the figure of authority to whom Sejosenye appeals—is powerless to comply with her request, much as he may wish to return her beautiful grandson to her. Devastated by her loss, Sejosenye succumbs to death soon afterwards.

There was a terrible moment on CNN on April 6th, 2007, when Virginia Tech police chief Wendell Flinchum confirmed the rumors swirling around the campus. Reporters asked him to approximate how many had been killed: more than twenty, he said. The room full of reporters, accustomed though they were to bad news, gasped. I gasped, too. Everything refused to behave normally after that. I believe I sat perfectly still on the sofa for several seconds repeating what he'd said. More than twenty? Impossible! Can't you return those words back?

I wanted to rush out of my house and into the street—turn left at the end of the driveway then left again onto Countryside Court, the road that had seemed pretty to me before but which ends in a cul-de-sac (something I should have remembered)—turn right onto North Main and run for two solid miles until I hit the mall—turn right at the chapel where I was married to a VT alumnus thirteen years before—skirt the Drill Field and hurry up the wide stone steps of Burruss Hall and find Chief Flinchum to demand that he return those words back to where they came from because how would we bear it if he didn't? How would parents tearing down I-81 in a futile effort to arrive in time to save their children begin to comprehend what had happened? How would they survive without their beautiful sons and daughters who had come to Virginia Tech to learn in safety with us?

Earlier that morning, I was sitting in my favorite chair, cradling my cup of tea. The tea was in a mug my husband, Larry, had ordered from some company online. A photo of my former executive assistant, Tammy Shepherd, and me had been glazed into the side. Tammy and I have our arms around each other's shoulders and we're grinning at the camera. We became friends during the four years when I served as chair of English. Tammy helped me wade through budget sheets and annual reports; she was a courageous ally when I was meeting with students who were in distress, insisting that she stay close by with her door open, even though I felt it may be risky for her to do so. "You don't have a choice," she would tell me. "I'm staying."

I was thinking about that evening's class. That semester, I was teaching my graduate poetry workshop on Mondays from 6:00P.M. to 8:45P.M. It had turned out to be one of the most enjoyable and fulfilling classes I had ever taught. Although I was still codirecting the Creative Writing program, I had stepped down from the position of chair of Virginia Tech's English department nearly a year before. Now that I was no longer responsible for overseeing a department of fifty professors, more than fifty instructors, seven classified staff, and dozens of graduate students, I had more time to devote to teaching. We were approaching the end of the semester and I needed to make sure that my comments on the drafts of the student poems were helpful.

Outside the weather was unseasonably-blustery, positively mean. A biting wind whipped the field behind our house, and the grass writhed with such synchronized beauty that it looked as if the entire field were underwater. There were even a few snow flurries. The walk from the car park to Shanks Hall where I taught the graduate workshop would be very chilly. I needed to remember to retrieve my winter coat from the back of the closet.

I had risen early that morning with a sense of foreboding. I knew exactly where it came from: I had been consumed with thoughts about Sierra Leone where I had taught at the age of twenty-one. Larry and I had visited the country at the end of 2006, hoping to form partnerships between Sierra Leone and Virginia Tech. It had been something of a personal pilgrimage. I needed to find out if students I had taught and a family with whom I had been close had survived the horrifying civil war. The ghosts from that country—the murdered villagers, the amputees who hobbled through the streets begging for food—populated my nightmares. I refused to accept the fact that, in all likelihood, most of the students I had taught as a young woman had been killed or had died by now. It had been nearly thirty years since then, and I hadn't been much older than they were. The average life span in Sierra Leone even before the war was around forty years old.

In preparation for our trip back to West Africa, I had read firsthand accounts of the slaughter and amputations by rebels and by children who had been forcibly conscripted into a juvenile army. The horror of what had transpired during a decade-long civil war made the infamous Children's Crusade seem like a day care excursion. But when we arrived in Sierra Leone we were greeted by some remarkable news: the family I had been close to had survived. All their children, including the one named after me, had survived also. The family had lost one grandchild. And although it looked likely that many of my former students and their families had not survived the war, some were living safely in places like Guinea or Mali, and a few were said to be in the United States. I had celebrated with old friends and promised new friends we met that we would find a way to do something constructive to help with the rebuilding process. I had an obligation to give something back because it was in Sierra Leone that I learned, like so many of Bessie Head's female characters, to find abiding joy in simple things. My African students were the ones who had reminded me how precious education was and how few people around the world had access to it. I had taught in Sierra Leone for two years as a volunteer in the United Kingdom's VSO program (Voluntary Service Overseas), the British equivalent of the Peace Corps. My Jamaican father had always told my English mother that Africa was home. He was right. In those two years in Sierra Leone I began to comprehend that lasting happiness could be wrung from very little.

Now that I was back in Blacksburg I had to work hard to keep my trip to Sierra Leone in the forefront of my imagination. The contrast between here and there was shocking, and the challenges posed by Sierra Leone's stuttering postwar economy were profound. It was difficult to know how best to partner with a country so impoverished that it lacked the most basic infrastructure. I had promised myself that I would find a way to do it, but I was concerned that I may have bitten off more than I could chew. The country was even less developed than it had been at the end of the seventies: a local currency that was almost worthless, no trustworthy banks or postal system, no credit cards (the banks in the country had been blacklisted because card numbers routed through the financial system were routinely stolen), appalling slums, a wounded populace, and a fragile government. And yet, in spite of all that, the resilience of the people was inspiring, and their friendliness touched me deeply. When I went back there, I had been welcomed like an old friend. Prior to our journey, Larry and I had joined forces with another professor at Virginia Tech, Ed Smith, who came from Sierra Leone. On a trip home himself, he had met us at Lunghi airport when we had visited. Having Ed as a guide made it a much more productive experience than it would otherwise have been. Upon our return to Blacksburg in January, I found solace in the serenity of the mountains and the peacefulness of the small college town. I had the luxury of recharging my batteries at Virginia Tech before returning refreshed to Sierra Leone for another visit.

I turned on CNN, something I have done habitually since 9/11. I was alone in the house. Larry, a computer systems network engineer and a classified staff person in the chemistry department at Virginia Tech, was working in the electronics shop in Davidson Hall. His office cubicle faces the Drill Field, the most recognizable feature of the Tech campus. He has a wonderful view out onto the center of campus at one side of the Drill Field, which functions as both hub and gathering place for students. The huge common area of grass and footpaths is where students throw Frisbees during the warmer months or hurry to class from their dorms located on the other side of the Drill Field from most of the classroom and administrative buildings. Burruss Hall dominates, with its castlelike appearance and its multicolored limestone façade, sitting majestically at the top of an imposing flight of stone steps. This is the seat of Virginia Tech's central administration—where the offices of the president, the provost, the treasurer, the vice presidents, the vice provosts, and other administrators are located.

Suddenly CNN was showing a map of Virginia. It took me a moment to realize that Blacksburg was being highlighted. Something was going on—a shooting incident on campus. Two people had been found dead.

The incident echoed a tragedy we had experienced eight months earlier. The previous August, on the first day of the fall semester, a gunman had been on the loose near campus. William Morva had shot and killed two people—hospital security guard Derrick McFarland on Sunday, August 20, and then, on Monday morning, Deputy Sheriff Eric Sutphin. He had also wounded another deputy sheriff. During that incident the administration had imposed a lockdown. It had been deemed too risky to do business as usual when no one knew exactly where the gunman was. Unaware that a gunman was on the loose, Larry and I had spent part of that August morning on an errand. We hadn't checked our email and so had no idea what was going on. As we had driven along deserted streets we had congratulated ourselves for selecting a time when no one was out and about.

The double homicide committed by William Morva had shaken the close-knit community. Although a crime like this was not unprecedented, it involved a resident who had been educated locally. A lot of people knew the perpetrator, and many knew the victims, so the crime touched a personal chord in the community.

By April 2007, a mere eight months had passed since the Morva shootings; they were still fresh in everyone's mind. Some of those who knew Morva claimed that he hadn't shown any sign of aggressive behavior. Others felt differently, telling reporters that he had made them decidedly uncomfortable.

The community responded to the tragedy in the way rural communities do when people in their midst have been harmed. There were benefits for the victims' families and memorial services. In smaller rural communities like Blacksburg and neighboring Christiansburg, each death is personal.

A gunman was on the loose again. It seemed as if we were about to relive what had become known as the "Morva incident." There were alarming reports coming into CNN of students hearing shots and seeing other students leaping from a classroom in Norris Hall. By now it was midmorning, the campus was in lockdown, and there were some horrifying rumors swirling around. Friends who monitored police channels were reporting a death toll that sounded too high to be credible. I reminded myself that people were prone to exaggeration during times of crisis. There had been bomb threats recently that had resulted in the closure off-campus. The threats had been left in three different buildings but had turned out to be hoaxes. Maybe these incidents were related.

The first two victims—who had originally been characterized by reporters as victims of "domestic violence" or a "murder-suicide"—had been found in West Ambler Johnston, a residence hall on the other side of the Drill Field from Burruss. The Virginia Tech administration had inexplicably delayed notifying the campus by email of the double homicide and the fact that a gunman could potentially be on the loose. My heart went out to the families and friends of the two dead students.

I called the English Department and spoke with Carolyn Rude, a close friend and the person who succeeded me as department chair. I also spoke with Tammy Shepherd, who was now serving as Carolyn's executive assistant. They were both on campus in Shanks and therefore in lockdown. I updated them about what I was hearing on the news. I flicked from CNN to WDBJ-7, the local channel out of Roanoke, which was doing a thorough job of covering the incident and already had reporters on the scene. I asked Tammy to find out if there were

English classes being taught over in Norris Hall. She checked the roster of classes. We were relieved to discover that there didn't seem to be any English faculty or TAs teaching in Norris that morning.

I called Larry. He was, as always, calm. "Don't go outside," I said to him needlessly. "They haven't found the shooter yet." Larry told me he could see the emergency personnel swarming towards Burruss. Ambulances and police cars were everywhere. "Stay away from the window!" I told him, furious that he was close enough to see anything.

The news was contradictory at first. In interviews with reporters, students spoke again of seeing people jumping from the windows of Norris Hall. The anchors on the local and national TV stations seemed to doubt these accounts, seemed to assume that the students were exaggerating. I can't recall the exact moment when I learned that this tragedy wasn't going to duplicate the one that had occurred in August, that it would be a grotesque enlargement of the homicides we'd seen then. But Virginia Tech police chief Wendell Flinchum wasn't the first to say the number twenty, just the first to confirm it. Hearing it from him was what made it real. Friends who had told it to friends who had recited the number to me over the phone could have been wrong. But now it was certain. The scale of the carnage was obscene.

I imagined how hard it must have been for Chief Flinchum to utter that phrase "more than twenty"— quite possibly harder to utter than any words he had uttered in his life. Wendell Flinchum had been promoted to the position of chief of the Virginia Tech Police Department (VTPD) just four months previously, in December 2006, having served in law enforcement for over twenty years. According to an article in the *Roanoke Times*, Flinchum had beaten out ninety-three other applicants for the position. He was described by one colleague, Lieutenant Vince Houston, as having "unbelievable" decision-making skills. "Even in a rushed situation, you know he's always thinking the next step." I watched Chief Flinchum as he tried to respond to the questions being hurled

at him from reporters. I had no doubt that this tragedy would haunt him because it had happened on
his watch. Some of those with guardianship respon-
sibilities are able to shake these things off, move on.
I felt instinctively that Chief Flinchum was not one of
those men. The horror of this day would never really
leave him. Like many others in the VTPD, he would
have died to protect the students.

I continued to make calls to see if people who I
thought could have been in Norris were safe, keeping
conversations as brief as possible because signals
were jammed due to the number of calls being made,
and people were having trouble getting through to
loved ones.

I left a voicemail message for my brother and
his family in Nottingham, England. I knew that this
news, given the possible scale of the killings, would
probably be broadcast in the United Kingdom. I
didn't want my family to learn about the shootings
from the television as I had. "We're fine," I lied to the
machine. "Larry's in lockdown, but he's fine."

I waited for Larry to return. I yearned to hear
the sound of the garage door because I knew it would
be the most merciful sound I would hear all day. I
paced back and forth waiting for his arrival, listening to fragments of news that seemed to come at me
like bludgeons, the horror of the disclosure causing
my head to ache the way it did during 9/11.

At last he arrived home. He was exiting the car
when I rushed into the garage. "More than twenty," I
said. He nodded. We held each other.

Throughout that day, the death toll rose. By
the time the first responders had counted the dead
in Norris Hall, the extent of the tragedy became
clear. Not twenty, but more than thirty dead. The
Virginia Tech president, Charles W. Steger, reserved
and clearly shaken, was right to call it "a tragedy of
monumental proportions."

It had taken law enforcement only three minutes to respond after they received a 911 call from
a student in Norris. Even though the three main
doors had been chained shut, they quickly found

an alternate entry and rushed into Norris Hall. And yet in spite of their swift response, there were dozens killed. The shooter had been ruthless, mowing down everyone in his path, turning classrooms into bloodbaths.

I continued watching TV, switching channels constantly, hoping to glean more information from the broadcasts. Anchors indicated with appalling insensitivity that the victim count would be a number for the record books, as if it were a worthy entry in Guinness World Records. There was some confusion about the title the gunman would claim. In those first few hours, it was already being billed as the largest death toll in an attack on a school in the United States until the Bath school disaster in Michigan in 1927 was found to have exceeded it. (The perpetrator in the Bath school disaster had utilized explosives as well as a rifle.) Later on, it became the largest mass murder by a single shooter. Each time I heard anchors and reporters talk about the record-breaking death toll I thought about those who were already titillated by violence and whose fantasies could now include a greater tally than before. The glorification of murder was in full swing. The final tally was thirty-three, including the gunman.

On CNN, a video from a student's cell phone was being played and replayed. The anchors exhorted us to listen carefully. If you did, you could hear the sound of a gun firing, like popcorn popping, a sound so innocent that it became even more sinister by contrast. The cell phone footage showed police surrounding the back of Norris Hall, approaching the building I had walked past a thousand times on my way to class or to a meeting. Law enforcement was breaking into the building from the other side. Usually it is pretty behind Norris—the landscaping crew takes great pride in the campus, especially in the buildings near the Drill Field. But today it looked like someone else's campus. It was like gazing down a well and seeing the image of a place you barely recognized trembling in the water below. Outside there were flurries of snow. It was not spring in Blacksburg, but winter. The sky was grim. The biting, blustery wind was so strong, they said, that the medical helicopters couldn't land. It was as if nothing, not even the weather, would ever be merciful anymore.

Early that afternoon I had received a call from an editor at the *New York Times*. Would I write an op-ed about how the tragedy had affected the community? It would appear in the next morning's paper. I agreed to do it. Over the years, I have trained myself to write my way through suffering—not to escape it, but instead to attempt to decipher my experience. I hadn't begun to understand the implications of the war in Sierra Leone until I had written a novel about it.

I wrote the op-ed in a single sitting. It took about forty minutes. Then I spent the next couple of hours revising it. As I faxed it to the editor at the New York Times I remember thinking, "There, it's done now." Writing it down had forced me to admit the horror to myself. Now there would be time to mourn.

I assumed I would be spending a large part of the rest of my career helping Virginia Tech, its students, staff, and faculty, come to terms with what had happened. This was my community, and I knew and loved dozens of people in it. I was devastated but I wasn't afraid. In fact, thinking that there were things I could do to help with the recovery process was one of the few consolations I had. Virginia Tech would reach out to the families and friends of the victims. We would come together in our grief and comfort each other. Foolishly, now that the worst had happened, I thought I was prepared for what was still to come.

When police revealed that the shooter was an Asian English major, a faculty member suggested to me over the phone that it could have been Seung-Hui Cho. I assured him he was mistaken. I was almost certain that the student I had known as "Seung" had graduated. And besides, I told him, there were many Asian students on campus. I shoved his suggestion to the back of my mind.

But on the morning of April 17, Virginia Tech released his name. A photo of Cho appeared on TV. And it was only then that I understood the depth of my own ignorance and felt the excruciating pain which comes with that realization.

The brooding young English major, the South Korean student who wanted to be a writer and whose presence seemed to mimic absence, was the one who had killed thirty-two people at Virginia Tech and then committed suicide. Something crumpled inside me. Now that I knew the identity of the shooter, sorrow was shot through with a new kind of anguish.

I had reported my concerns about this student to various units across campus, letting them know that he seemed depressed and angry. I had worked with him myself when it seemed there was no other viable alternative. I had struggled to get him into counseling. Eventually, if what he had told me was true—and now I had no reason to believe that it was—he had contacted the on-campus counseling center. But even if he had been telling me the truth and had sought help, it hadn't made a scrap of difference in the end.

In the first two days following the shootings, I began to learn that Seung-Hui Cho had produced writing more disturbing than the samples I had seen, and much of it had been written after I had stepped down from serving as chair. An example of a play he had written was posted on the Net by someone who had been in a playwriting class with him in the fall of 2006. Had Seung-Hui Cho modified his rhetoric when he had met with me? Why hadn't I realized that he could be the killer before it was officially confirmed that this was the case? I was known to be someone who could make her voice heard, someone people listened to, one of the most vocal people at Virginia Tech. But the efforts I had made had been futile. All those people dead.

I had been on research leave last semester. Had Seung-Hui Cho attempted to see me and found my office door closed? Had he looked for me again this semester, by which time I had mistakenly thought he had graduated? I was desperate for time to digest what had happened.

But there wasn't any time for reflection—no time to think before the next decision needed to be made. An email had been sent to all Virginia Tech employees informing us that anyone who had information about the tragedy should contact the police. I conferred with Carolyn Rude, and we called faculty members in English who had taught Cho and advised them to call the police and let them know that they had taught him. I told them that any material they had about him should be handed over at once to authorities. I had material to hand over myself—emails I had written to various units around campus expressing my concern about him, copies of the work he'd shared with me, and the emails he himself had sent.

But before I had time to gather much of anything, the phone began to ring. Apart from the hours between 11:00 P.M. and 6:00 A.M., it didn't stop ringing for the next few days.

Reporters from newspapers, television, and radio all wanted to know whether or not it was true that I had tutored Seung-Hui Cho. I was fielding calls from across the United States, the United Kingdom, South Korea, and Canada. Could I confirm that I had warned the administration about him? When I asked them how they had found out about this they told me that my name and the details of my association with Cho had been given to them by a faculty member. I had thought that I had conveyed to those who knew about my contact with Seung-Hui Cho that questions from the media needed to be routed through University Relations, standard practice at the university. But I also realized that the pressure being placed on everyone by the media was intense. I reasoned it was quite possible that University Relations had routed them back to me.

I wasn't sure how to handle the media. I called the office of Larry Hincker, who was associate vice president for University Relations and the university spokesperson. I left an urgent message with his assistant asking for advice. I tried to imagine how I would feel if I had lost a son or daughter in the shootings. I had not been close to those who were killed, though I had, of course, known the person who had murdered them.

The thought of becoming known as Seung-Hui Cho's teacher weighed heavily on me, and I knew I would be obliged to carry this burden for the rest of my life. I would be questioned about it, forced to relive the association. But it seemed to me there was no choice. Having learned about Cho's furtiveness I was sick of secrets. There were those to whom I had appealed who had done their best to assist me. I would explain that their hands had been tied by privacy laws and by Virginia Tech's policies. I would not give out anyone else's name because I knew that would make them vulnerable. Had I known on April 17 as the phone rang off the hook and the reporters hammered on the door that my decision to answer questions would have so many lasting repercussions I would still have felt morally obliged to respond.

There was no word from Larry Hincker's office, and the reporters hadn't let up. I decided it was best to ask the media if they would leave if I responded to their questions all at once, talking with them as a group. I needed to get up to campus, and dodging their questions would mean I had to face them later. My husband ventured outside and asked them if they would be willing to abide by these terms, and they agreed. It didn't take long to speak with them, and those who were present honored our agreement.

Hastily, I put together a file of all the papers I could lay my hands on and hurried to Burruss Hall where the investigation was headquartered. Larry and I drove to campus, which was heavily guarded. We were stopped by security, but when we said we were Tech employees and were going to hand things over to the police, we were permitted to drive around the Drill Field to Burruss Hall. At the doors of Burruss we were greeted again by security. We were ushered into the president's suite on the second floor where we ran into Provost Mark McNamee and his wife, Carole. Both were clearly devastated by what had happened. We embraced each other.

I noticed out of the corner of my eye that there was a young girl, who I assumed was a student, sitting on one of the sofas in the reception area. She was crying softly. Everyone, it seemed, was crying today. Before I could say anything to her, Larry and I were whisked off down a corridor. I was shown into a room I couldn't recall seeing before—probably someone's office—while Larry waited outside. I handed over my file to the officer. It consisted mostly of a series of emails written to people who worked in Student Affairs, the Cook Counseling Center, the College of Liberal Arts and Human Sciences, and the VTPD. I had included any work I could find by Seung-Hui Cho. Because my notes about the student had been copied to a number of people, I told the officer that this material would duplicate other material he would be receiving, or had already received, but I thought it wise to share it with him nevertheless.

The interview was very brief and, to my surprise, the officer didn't have any questions for me, though he did take the file. I asked him if I needed to speak with anyone else, and he said they would call me if they needed to talk to me. I met again with law enforcement on April 23 because I was concerned about a related security issue, but apart from a couple of other instances when I called the FBI to talk about concerns I had about the case, my interactions with them were over. Although it surprised me that they did not have more questions about Cho, I also understood that the FBI, the Bureau of Alcohol, Tobacco, Firearms and Explosives (KIF), and state and local police had thirty-two homicides and one suicide to investigate. The amount of work they would be doing to prepare the campus for the return of the students, faculty, and staff would be enormous. Before I left, I tried to impress upon the officer that I would be more than willing to assist with the investigation in any way possible. I believe it was later that day when a friend told me that the student who had been crying in President Steger's reception area was blaming herself for what happened. Apparently she had been in a class with Cho and noticed his strange behavior but she hadn't reported it. From that moment on, every time I spoke about what had happened I tried to keep her in mind. She needed to understand that she was not to blame.

Soon afterwards, Nikki Giovanni, a university distinguished professor and faculty member in the English Department, came forward and spoke to the media. Once she did, I acknowledged that she had been the professor who had reported her concerns to me about SeungHui Cho in October 2005. She had also shared with me a poem of his that she found particularly disturbing. I was grateful to her for stepping forward, and grateful, too, that she had voiced her concerns to me about Cho in the first place. If I hadn't been told that his writing and behavior were troubling, I may not even have realized he was an English major until after the shootings. We have about five hundred majors and around two hundred minors in English, and we serve many thousands of students in other majors. It would have been easy to miss him. Even though my efforts ended up being futile, the fact that Nikki had notified me about his work and behavior had at least given me the opportunity to reiterate my concerns about troubled students, and to try to get Cho into counseling.

It took many days before things calmed down enough for me to begin to take stock of what had happened; weeks before I realized how harsh the penalty would be for speaking out; months more before I had the strength to begin sifting through the horror story he crafted with himself in the starring role.

On April 20, Cho's sister, Sun-Kyung Cho, issued a statement, part of which is excerpted here:

On behalf of our family, we are so deeply sorry for the devastation my brother has caused. No words can express our sadness that 32 innocent people lost their lives this week in such a terrible, senseless tragedy. We are heartbroken.

We grieve alongside the families, the Virginia Tech community, our State of Virginia, and the rest of the nation. And the world . . .

We are humbled by this darkness. We feel hopeless, helpless and lost. This is someone that I grew up with and loved. Now I feel like I didn't know this person.

We have always been a close, peaceful and loving family. My brother was quiet and reserved, yet struggled to fit in. We never could have envisioned that he was capable of such violence. He has made the world weep.

I think of Sun-Kyung and her family. Branded by Cho's actions, they cannot simply grieve; they have to assume the burden he has willed to them. Unable to compete with his Princeton-educated sister in life, Cho has triumphed over her in death. Sun-Kyung Cho will spend much of the rest of her life apologizing for something she did not do.

Her words are so full of anguish that they seem to tremble on the page. I cannot imagine how she will have the strength to carry her grief.

It is October 2005, eighteen months before the mass shootings at Virginia Tech.

The young man called Seung-Hui Cho enters my office in sunglasses and a cap. He sits down and speaks in the softest voice I have ever heard coming from a full-grown man; it is so soft in fact that I have to lean forward to hear him. He has already tried to persuade some of us in the English Department that we have misunderstood him—that he isn't angry at all, that we overreacted to the disturbing poem he wrote, a poem he claims was meant to make us laugh.

T. S. Eliot was right: April is the cruelest month.

Bessie Head was right, too: some things can never be taken back.

Matthew Vollmer

NeVer ForgeT

No one now living knows much about the massacre at Draper's Meadow. No witness to the events ever penned an account, and most—if not all—renderings of the events can be traced to a couple of reports written by descendants of the victims. We don't know the exact location of the massacre, though it's safe to say that it occurred on land that is now a part of the campus of Virginia Tech, most likely in the vicinity of the Duck Pond, a place Blacksburg residents now visit to seek solace: to fish for mud bass, to feed mallards and Muscovy and Canadian geese, to stroll paths creased with frost heaves, to stare at rippling water. Nor do we know what motivated the band of Shawnee Indians to attack this place, once home to a group of enterprising trans-Alleghany pioneers. The explanation given by John Ingles, a descendant of one of the survivors, who claimed that the Shawnee were simply quenching "a heathen thirst for bloodshed and plunder," smacks of the prevailing attitudes that justified the denigration—and thus persecution—of an entire country's worth of indigenous people. And while the Shawnee might have had any number of reasons for attacking this particular settlement—after all, the whites here had begun farming land that, by some accounts, had once been sacred hunting grounds—it's also possible that the Indians had targeted Draper's Meadow because the French, as part of their new alliance against the British at the outset of the French and Indian Wars, had promised compensation for the scalps of Englishmen. This premise is especially alluring when one considers that the victims of the attack included Colonel James Patton, a formidable—if somewhat arrogant and opportunistic—Irish sea captain and frontiersman, who, in his dealings with Indians and whites alike, had made a good many enemies, and who—it is presumed—had broken away from a supply train to pause at Draper's Meadow, possibly for recuperative purposes.

We don't know which settler spotted the Indians first. We're told that Mrs. George Draper, who sounded the initial alarm, ran into her cabin to retrieve her baby, only to be shot in the arm as she fled. She subsequently dropped her infant child, whom the Shawnee scooped up and whose head they dashed against the ends of cabin logs. Should we believe that Colonel Patton, described by others as "robust" and "Herculean," was sitting at a writing desk in one of the primitive dwellings when he heard Mrs. Draper's warning cry? That he grabbed his broadsword and strode out the cabin's front door, where, before being shot dead, he struck down two of his attackers? We don't know how the Indians slew their remaining victims, or whether they scalped them. We know only that some died, while others—perhaps those who appeared to be in better shape, and could therefore help replenish the recently diminished Shawnee population—were taken captive, one of whom happened to be Mary Draper Ingles, whose story of escaping the tribe once they reached Ohio and returning to Virginia on foot, alongside an old Dutch woman who may or may not have tried to eat her—*twice*—is a tale often told in these mountains. We know the Indians set fire to the buildings, but we're unclear about how they did so, whether they arrived bearing torches or used fireplace logs already burning. We're told that the Indians' last act, subsequent to setting the settlement ablaze, was to decapitate a man named Philip Barger and to deliver a sack containing his head to Mrs. Philip Lybrook, who lived in a cabin with her husband at the mouth of Sinking Creek. Did the Shawnee speak English, and did they, as legend has it, instruct Mrs. Lybrook to look inside the bag, in order to "find someone she knew"? How much time passed before William Ingles and John Draper—husbands of Draper and Mary Ingles, who escaped capture or death by working in the nearby wheat fields—looked up from their work and saw smoke rising above the trees? No one can say. We don't know if any of the victims were still alive once these men reached the settlement—if these farmers braved flumes of heat to drag their friends and loved ones away from the fire, or if instead they had to wait until the bodies were long dead and aswarm with green iridescent flies before they could retrieve them.

One of the few things we do know for sure is that no trace of these settlers' cabins remains. When I say "we," it's not even clear what I mean. The massacre, which I've rarely, if ever, heard anyone talk about, has been largely forgotten. The majority of Blacksburg's current residents seem largely unaware of the event. It's true that a number of historical markers commemorate the event but these markers are hard to find. There's a tarnished metal plate, upon which has been engraved a dedication to those who lost their lives on that day, bolted to a rock embedded in the ground on a hillock not far from the university's President's House. A stone ledge, buried in the earth on the northeast side of the Duck Pond, bears the following words: DRAPER'S MEADOW MASSACRE, JULY 8, 1755. It's easy to imagine visitors reading this inscription and having no idea what to make of it, of bypassing the phrase "DRAPER'S MEADOW" and the date, and zeroing in on the word "MASSACRE," and that particular series of letters delivering them to an altogether different time and place.

On the morning of April 16, 2007, more than a quarter of a millennium later, the weather is lousy. I am out in it: jogging through a blizzard of stinging flakes to a bus stop, on my way to the Virginia Tech campus, where I teach creative writing and composition. The snow churns in gusts, seems never to land, fails to accumulate. Once aboard the bus, I hook my arm around a silver post, and we lurch forward, a packed crew of mostly sleepy undergraduates, whose shampoo and cologne smell perfumes the air. A sullen, chubby girl eats Cheerios from a plastic bag. Another, slowly chewing gum, types on her phone with her thumbs. I stare at the patchy beard of a droopy-lidded guy who suddenly yawns so intensely it appears he might be in danger of dislocating his jaw.

What I don't know, what nobody else on this bus knows: two people have been shot in a dormitory on the west side of campus. These people are now dying; perhaps they are already dead. Had someone announced this news to the bus, riders would've surely murmured or winced or lifted their eyebrows. Some would've cursed, drawn the words out in slow exhalations, holy this or holy that, flipped open a phone to check the news. But the bus would've kept going. It wouldn't have turned around. Nobody would've gotten off at the next stop, because nobody ever gets off at the next stop—somebody always gets on. Those students who were headed to the building where, in less than half an hour, hundreds of bullets will be fired into the bodies of forty-seven people, would not have recharted their courses. They would have continued onward. Even had they known, they would have hoped that the people who'd been shot were okay and that the police would apprehend the shooter. They would have remembered the schizophrenic homeless man from the beginning of the year, the one who'd shot an officer on the Huckleberry Trail, the ribbon of asphalt leading from downtown Blacksburg to the New River Valley Mall, in Christiansburg. They would have assumed—as I surely would have—that by the time we reached campus, someone, somewhere, would have things under control.

The bus stops at McBryde Hall, one building from Norris, the site where Sueng Hui Cho will fire 170 rounds into the bodies of forty-seven students and faculty. I walk a hundred yards east, enter Shanks Hall, and climb four flights of stairs to my office, where I pour coffee from a thermos into a thermos cap and check my email and then work on a story I've been writing about a dentist whose wife dies on his honeymoon, following an allergic reaction to a manta ray sting. I break from the story and I'm listening to a band called Deerhunter on the computer as I read the last chapters of *American Pastoral*, a novel by Phillip Roth that concerns a guy named Swede, a former high school basketball star who takes over his father's glove factory and marries Miss New Jersey and produces a daughter who later becomes a domestic terrorist.

Wife who dies. Hunter. Domestic terrorist. I fail to note the thematic connection between these words, and thus the synchronicity fails to make itself known. A beep sounds; I click a postage stamp on my screen. The email, from University Relations, explains that a "shooting incident" has occurred and that everyone at Tech should contact the VT Police if they spot anything "suspicious." Word in the building is that it's a drug deal gone bad and that the shooter's been identified as a student from nearby Radford University. *Whatever,* I think, and return—relatively unconcerned—to my reading. The book's amazing; I'm completely absorbed. Twenty-five minutes later, another email: "A gunman is loose on campus. Stay in buildings until further notice." *Whoa,* I think. *Crazy.* I shut my book, close my office door, call my wife, Kelly, who tells me to be careful. I check the *Roanoke Times* website and CNN and *Washington Post*. Nothing.

A megaphone system announces, "This is an emergency. Seek shelter immediately. Stay away from windows." I immediately disobey this command, wheeling my chair to my window, which looks out onto a dormitory and a slice of Turner Street, and the Burger King on the other side. A couple of ambulances speed past. I am not alarmed. I don't think, *Those are for the dead and dying.*

Three girls, wearing coats and pajama bottoms, emerge from the dorm next door. They light cigarettes. They yell something incomprehensible and defiant. They laugh.

They don't yet know.

Neither do I.

The first number I hear is one. Then three. Then twenty. *Twenty* students. *Killed.* Professors, grad students, and stunned undergraduates who obeyed the commands of the public-address system begin to emerge from offices, whispering huskily. Should we stay? Is it over? Finally somebody says, "I don't know about y'all but I'm getting the hell outta here."

I follow a professor—a tall, thin man with hunched shoulders and horn-rimmed glasses, who has agreed to give me a ride home. Nobody told us we were free to leave, nobody knows if we need permission, nobody knows if it—whatever "it" is—is over. On the way to the parking lot, I feel exposed, permeable. I brace myself for the sting of a sniper's bullet, the pop of gunfire. I eye every stranger we pass, and every distant figure, with suspicion. I tell myself to act normal—whatever that means. It's like one of those dreams I have where I find myself in a public place without clothes, or I've forgotten to wear pants, but I've convinced myself that I can survive the situation by acting like nothing is wrong. By the time we reach the parking lot, my pulse has quickened. Inside the professor's car, I have to fight the urge to slump to the floor, or at least below the window. I glance into the rearview mirror, where the professor's eyes are wide, bulging as he slides his key into the ignition. His face is pale and expressionless. He says, "This is huge. This is big-time. Everybody's going to know somebody."

In my head I fill in the words he omitted: *who has died.*

At home, Kelly and I lock our doors and windows. We still don't know whether what's happened is over, and as absurd as it would seem for the shooter to end up inside our house, we aren't taking any chances. Problem is, our family's incomplete: Elijah, our three-year-old son, is still in preschool. We debate whether we should walk past the cul-de-sac at the end of the street and then through a stand of pine trees and then across another street to the Church of the Brethren and retrieve him. We've heard that all schools in the county are on lockdown. We also know that, during the day, the doors of the church remain unlocked, and that—under normal circumstances—anybody can stroll right in. We tell ourselves that Elijah will be safe there, in rooms stacked to the ceiling with board games and Tupperware containers of toys, a place where the white-bearded Mr. Bungard and the white-haired Ms. Noni, with their extraordinary powers of persuasion, are able to convince a dozen three-year-olds to quietly eat their snacks, while sitting upon a single blanket, all facing the same direction. We assume our fear is unwarranted, but still, we would like to bring him home, to lock and dead-bolt the doors and hold him, to know for sure that he's safe—despite the fact that he is not the kind of child who really wants to be held, mainly because he refuses to sit still. In the end, we defer to the judgment of Ms. Noni, who tells us over the phone that there's no reason to interrupt him, that he's playing happily with his friends. We postpone our retrieval and pray we're doing the right thing.

We watch TV with our laptops open, refreshing CNN and Fox and the *New York Times*. Our inboxes have been flooded with email. We field calls, try to return messages, but it's difficult; we keep losing signals. The wind's insane—too strong, we learn, for helicopters to airlift wounded. Lights blink. Clocks flash wrong times. The TV goes black, then bursts suddenly to life. Each time, the clamor startles us.

We flip channels, seeking eyewitness accounts. We want a justification, however absurd. We want to know how and why this happened, and who was responsible. But we also want names. We need to know if anyone we know was among those who were injured or slain.

I picture the faces of my students and am overcome by an unexpected and desperate fondness for each one, regardless of how much grief they've given me: Jessica, the blond Republican who campaigned the previous semester for a state senator; John, the meek speed-metal guitarist; Matt, the droopy-lidded stoner; Brendan, a kid who unironically loves Carnival Cruises; the girl with the last name Butt; the guy with the last name Christ.

Some respond to my emails. Most say they're okay; others aren't sure. Some know people who were shot, others are waiting to hear back. All are shocked and horrified but thankful someone's asked how they are. I imagine entering the classroom but can't get past that. I can't imagine asking them to narrow research questions, choose a genre, construct a thesis statement.

The final count is thirty-two—thirty-three, if you're feeling generous enough to count the shooter. Many aren't. And don't.

The victims include a former coffeehouse singer, a master's student researching the sustainability of water quantity during drought, a triple major who played the baritone in the band, an effervescent French teacher, a skilled horsewoman, an accomplished swimmer, a triathlete who also happened to be a top researcher in biomechanics, a master's student researching storm-water management, a residence-hall adviser who cared for her residents as if she were their mother, a teaching assistant who'd been credited for discovering the first West Nile virus–infected mosquito in Centre County, an accomplished classical pianist with dreams of studying nanotechnology, an award-winning engineering student, a member of the cadet jazz band, a Ph.D. student in civil engineering, a world-renowned hydrologist, and a holocaust survivor.

The accompanying photos showcase the

obliviousness of innocence. Studying them, reading the biographies, I can't help but wonder if Norris Hall was an arbitrary choice on the part of the shooter, or if he'd done his research and targeted the building that held the highest percentage of the university's overachievers and said to himself, *Yes*, this *will be my final destination.*

At the entrances to our buildings, signs appear—not paper signs but plastic ones, maroon letters that read: MEDIA PLEASE RESPECT OUR MOURNING. This is, for the media, an impossible request to honor. Mourning is a main staple of the media's diet, and therefore what it continuously hunts. The media, when it asks how we're doing, hopes our answer is "Not well." The media snakes its tentacles into the cracks of a tragedy, feeling, probing, asking: *What can I find? Is it sharp enough? Dangerous enough? Sad enough?* If the answer is yes, then it slaps on its suckers, shows it to anyone who will watch, moves to the next thing.

Let me be clear: I'm one of those watchers. In fact, I seem to be defined at this moment only by my insatiable need to consume news coverage. For hours I flip between channels, worried that I'm on the wrong one, that the one I'm not watching is the one broadcasting the information I need. I learn that Professor Libriscu barricaded the door with his body so students could line up at the windows and leap out; that Kevin Granata tried to tackle the gunman; that a girl who'd been shot twice in the head had survived by playing dead, hiding her phone in her hair as she whispered to 911 dispatch; that the cell phones of dead students were ringing inside body bags as responders lugged them from the building. I am absorbing more information than I know what to do with. My head feels like it's housing a snowstorm of static. My eyes burn. I flit between channels and browser windows. I don't know what I'm looking for. It's too early to accept the truth: that no amount of information will explain what has happened.

Meanwhile, the campus has become a prop, a setting, a backdrop for a particular kind of event: the media-glutted aftermath. "Here we are at Virginia Tech," the reporters say, "the scene of the largest mass murder in American history." The largest. The worst. The deadliest. The tragedy is, they insist, something that can—and must—be measured. They might as well be saying: *Here we are at the worst thing of all time.*

The *V* and *T* accompanying the headlines begin to look foreboding—like the blunt ends of instruments that might be used to bludgeon someone. Cable-news stations have created special logos for this story. The *Virginia Tech* in *Virginia Tech Massacre* appears to be the logo of a corporate sponsor, as though the massacre was an event subsidized by the school.

A reporter tells a student—one who appears on several different channels in the same gray Virginia Tech sweatshirt, a kid who helped engineer the barricading of a door that the shooter tried but failed to enter after blasting two holes through it—that some are calling him a hero. What does the student think of that? The student tries to speak, but can't. His face contracts; he's trying to stop himself from crying.

He quenches a couple of sobs, squeaks out: "I'm just glad to be here." He's happy to still be alive. It's the only thing he knows for sure.

The anchorman of Headline News says, "Mm." He jerks once in his chair, the way a dead body might were it to receive a sudden surge of electricity. "Raw emotion," he says, as if naming something foreign, a phenomenon he's read about, and can therefore only imagine.

Two days after the shootings, Kelly and I attend a convocation, which is held in Cassel Coliseum, the university's basketball arena. By the time we arrive, the coliseum's full. Along with the rest of the overflow crowd, we're directed to neighboring Lane Stadium, where we sit under a blazing sun, a sky now blue.

Every fall, fans congregate here to eat monolithic turkey legs and cheer the Hokie defense as it incapacitates opponents. Now the face of the President of the United States appears on the screen of the Jumbotron. It is the head of a man who, four years earlier, supported the preemptive invasion of a country that posed a theoretical threat to our national security. Depending on which statistical records you believe, this invasion may have killed and wounded as many as hundreds of thousands of innocent people. The head, which attempts to look serious, says that it is filled with sorrow, and that someday, whether we can picture it now or not, things will return to normal.

Members of the Virginia Tech administration take turns saying things they think we want to hear, or perhaps things they want to hear themselves say. A poet, our most famous, stands to speak. She wears a black suit, a white shirt, a loose black tie. She begins with an assessment—"We are sad today"—and ends with a prophecy: "We will prevail." *Wait*, I think. Why are we already thinking about prevailing? Didn't the shootings happen only two days ago? Weren't they still happening, in some sense? Weren't we reliving them in our waking and sleeping dreams?

The Jumbotron is malfunctioning, its words now indecipherable. Everything sounds like it's underwater, like it's been reverbed and delayed. The sun—a brutal light—bears down on us. We exit the stadium thirsty and sunburnt. On the way out, I pick up a *Collegiate Times* newspaper. On the back page, Lockheed Martin—the largest manufacturer of weaponry in the world, and a company who has offered significant philanthropic support to Virginia Tech's engineering program—has printed its condolences.

In other news, auditions for *Girls Gone Wild* have been canceled.

At our departmental meeting, the room is packed: TAs, professors, faculty I've never seen before. I wonder who had the shooter in class, who knew him, who feels responsible. I wonder who refuses to feel responsible, since what could he or she have really done when faced with a person who'd nurtured such monstrous desires?

Refreshments—seven-layer dip, Fritos, pound cake—have been arranged on a folding table. Representatives from Human Resources take turns at a podium: a tall guy with a radio voice, a man who looks like he could play a doctor on TV, a woman who apologizes for being soft-spoken. We collect handouts that include the phrase *grief management*. A woman said to be an authority in these matters informs us that we should engage in something creative. We might find it comforting, she says, to do something with our hands. We might find solace in gardening. I clench my jaw and shake my head, not at the idea of finding solace, but at the idea that the institution would presume to tell us where it might be found.

After the meeting, Kelly and I decide to take a walk through campus. We exit Shanks—the building that houses our department—and for the first time the building's name on the signage outside suggests to me homemade weaponry. I do not mention this to Kelly. I don't say anything and neither does she.

We pass Norris, the building where the shootings took place. Police tape thrashes in the wind outside. What does it look like in there? Are there people scrubbing bloodstains? Reporters wander the Drill Field, interviewing students, who themselves are wandering. Classes have been canceled. The building: it was full of classrooms where students doodled and snoozed, jotted notes or drew graffiti. The question was now: when people have been shot and killed there—people you knew, or knew of, or didn't know—where should you go? Everywhere seems like the wrong place to be. The students flock to Kentucky Fried Chicken. They nap on the floor of the local Blockbuster. They place stuffed animals wearing little T-shirts with VT logos upon makeshift shrines. They stand blinking and cold before great waxen candle blobs that rarely flicker with light because the wind keeps blowing them out. They hold signs that say FREE HUGS AND HERSHEY KISSES. They enter great blue-and-white striped tents tethered to the Drill Field to view dozens of long white wooden boards bearing thousands of messages:

> *NeVer ForgeT.*
> *I never knew any of you. I will miss you all.*
> *There are 32 angels in heaven today explaining*
> *   what a HOKIE is.*
> *32 gone. Because 1 was lost.*
> *Dear Cho, Sleep in peace and let the all the*
> *things that hurt you a lot go.*
> *I'm sorry I couldn't do more.*

I too feel compelled to write something, to put my name upon one of these gigantic sympathy cards that will later be archived in University Storage. The problem is that I have no idea what to write. I'm crippled by self-consciousness and the knowledge that anything I could possibly write would be laughably inadequate. It is futile to address the dead. Brash to make pronouncements. Presumptuous to make public my own private and conflicted sentiments. And why, of all things, would my *sentiments* matter? All that matters is that the sons and daughters of mothers and fathers, those who were once the age of my own son, are now gone forever. No amount of never forgetting will bring them back.

Our wandering brings us to the Inn at Virginia Tech, where skirted banquet tables offer faux-silver platters of granola bars and snack cakes, bowls of apples and oranges and bananas—nourishment for the grieving, for those who are investigating the source of the grief, and for those reporting it. A wall-sized screen in a conference room plays news footage, which, when we pass it, features a still photo of the shooter. His head, which fills the screen, is at least a half a story tall. It has spoken more since it perished than it did during the past twenty-two years.

There are no answers to our questions—only facts. The shooter wrote stories and plays and poems about sexual abuse and violence. He had an imaginary girlfriend named "Jelly." He refused to speak. He said that he didn't have a choice: he had to kill. He said someone could've stopped him. He wanted to be referred to as a question mark.

In another conference room, two hundred people are being debriefed. Earlier, a psychologist explained how to stop yourself from crying during television interviews: move your fingers and toes. This physical activity, she said, would trick your brain, and stop your tears. Now, someone's reading names from the list of the injured, none of which I recognize. Are the people in this room family members of the victims? If so, I feel bad that we've intruded. And yet I don't know what else to do. I feel terrible if I take my mind off the shooter and victims. I feel terrible if I keep my mind on the shooter and the victims. Feeling terrible, it seems, is my new vocation, one that—despite how easy it seems—I feel like I'm failing.

I feel disconnected and empty and ashamed for wanting to feel something other than what I do, part of which is: *I could've been there.* If I'd been there, if I'd borne witness, I'd have earned the right to wonder why I'd survived, why I—and not others—had been spared. Not to be dead and yet not to be a survivor, either—and not to know personally anyone who died—was not to know one's place in the tragedy. You were there but you weren't. You'd forever be associated with a disaster you hadn't experienced, a storm whose epicenter remained hidden. You'd feel sad but not sad enough. You'd want to grieve but not be able to—and it'd feel false if you did.

On our way back from the inn, we're stopped by an adolescent girl with dark curly hair. She introduces herself and her brother, a younger red-head with freckles, and asks if we know that God loves us, asks if we know that if we died today, we would go to heaven.

It doesn't take long for me to realize what's happened: our campus has been identified as a place touched by evil and in need of comfort. It has become a setting where opportunistic young evangelists can come to save souls. I received an email from a relative the day before, telling me how proud he was of his church's response to the tragedy, which occasioned an email of my own, to my unsuspecting mother, in which I typed the following rant: *What kind of world is he living in where he feels the need to express "pride" for booklets presented as self help devices but which are actually doctrine delivery devices? . . . People are grieving here. Truly grieving. If he thinks this is a chance to indoctrinate people, he is truly out of touch with reality.*

A hundred yards farther on from the curly-haired girl, we're interrupted by another woman. She's wearing a brown velour tracksuit. She has bleached blonde hair. Pink lips. Tan skin. Diamond necklace. She also wants to know whether we know that if we died today we would go to heaven.

What we tell her: "No, thanks."

Some students claim that they tried to befriend Cho. To greet him. To include him. Maybe they did. Maybe they didn't. Maybe they're saying this in order to evade responsibility, to make themselves feel better. Hey, they think, I tried saying hi to him, I tried talking to him and he wouldn't talk, he wouldn't speak. I wonder, though, if anyone called him out. Where were the young evangelists when Cho needed a friend? Where was someone to say, "Hey, Cho, you know what, this act you're putting on—this farcical, existential, I'm-tormented-and-won't-speak act—is total bullshit." What if someone had dedicated time to being Cho's friend? *You know that guy who never speaks? I'm pouring all my energy into him, I'm*

*going to make him better, and I'm going to say to him,
You aren't unlovable, people don't hate you, they just
maybe think you don't speak English, or that you're
shy, or that you're psycho. Are you psycho? Because
it's okay to be psycho, as long as you don't hurt anybody or yourself. I'm going to love you if it kills me.*

At noon the next day, hundreds of students and
faculty—all wearing orange and maroon—stream
into the Drill Field for a memorial service. A makeshift memorial in front of Burrus Hall features thirty-
two limestone slabs, each one piled with flowers and
stuffed animals and candles and laminated photos:
faces of the slain. Balloons bearing the school colors
are released; they fly away until they are tiny dots in
the sky, until my brain is tricking me into thinking I
still see them when I can no longer be sure. A chap-
lain reads the full name of each victim, after which
a bell is rung. This happens thirty-two times. I lose
count, think it's never going to end. How long will
the dead be remembered? Will people memorialize
this tragedy 250 years from now?

For weeks, our school exists at the epicenter of
a place in history, a supercharged moment in an absurd world, a world whose semi trucks are delivering
shipments of teddy bears, handmade quilts, framed
photographs, memorial ribbons, memory books,
paper chains and handwritten letters. Inside the
Squires Student Center, the walls have been draped
with plastic banners bearing the logos of other uni-
versities. They're like giant flexible cards markered
with the names of well-wishers and people who are
keeping Hokies in their thoughts and prayers. I
pause to read some, wondering, "Do they mean me?
Am I a Hokie?" Everybody from everywhere seems to
be repeating the same chants: "We are keeping you
in our thoughts and prayers" and "We are all Hokies
today." I wonder who made these banners, what kind
of person organizes or even knows to organize something like this, and why a banner, and who has the
energy and the unself-consciousness and generosity

to do such a thing, to write, *We Will Prevail*, and then sign one's name.

I go for a run. At the halfway mark I trip on a frost heave in the asphalt, fall, scrape the palms of my hands. The endorphins, the pain, the sight of blood—and the phrase *blood on my hands* actually appears in my mind. I'm afraid to wipe the blood on my sleeves, as I'm wearing my new Hokies shirt. I don't know what else to do but brush myself off and keep running. But when I try to move, I can't. I'm hyperventilating. I'm crying. It feels good. I'm sad when it passes. I would like to cry more, but whatever grief I feel is buried in a well that's too deep to tap.

Undergraduates gather in Shanks for treats: a plate of ham, finger sandwiches, Cokes, brownies. But nobody eats. A tall, angular professor hoists a tray and totes it around the room, accepting refusals of food with a gracious nod. Our famous poet sits at a table, signing copies of the poem she read at the convocation, copies of which the department is distributing to English majors. The line to get the poem signed leads out the door and down the hall. I ask Hannah, a former student, how she's doing. She rolls her eyes. "This sucks," she says. I ask if she's going to get her poem signed. "Yeah," she says, "I'm gonna be like, Will you sign my depressing keepsake?" I laugh but instantly catch myself.

I still don't know what to do with the phrase *We will prevail*—three words that have already been transformed into signage, emblazoned upon the back windows of Blazers and Explorers and Range Rovers like so many talismans. I worry about the "we." I worry it's not true. Will we *all* prevail? Maybe not. Certainly most will. Most need to know that someone they love and trust believes they have the power to move on. Most need to know this won't happen again, that our school is still safe and fun and awesome, that it can't be changed, that the phrase

Virginia Tech won't be resurrected only with the word *massacre*.

But what about the rest? What about the some? Some lost their one and onlys, their favorites. Some lost the loves of their lives, their fathers and mothers and brothers and sisters. Some will toil in darkness— for years—and never recover. Some can't, and won't, be inspired. The eyes of some won't get watery when ESPN plays lonely trumpet music over a montage of VT photos before sporting events, because they're not watching sporting events, especially not those that take place at Virginia Tech. Some see *NeVer ForgeT* bumper stickers and avert their eyes, because "never forget"—for some—sounds like a curse.

My son—three years old—is asleep. My son, I'd like to report, has a cherubic face. Then again, most children do, especially when sleeping. Years earlier, the parents of the slain gazed upon their own sleeping toddlers and presumed those faces to be cherubic. These parents reflected already on the passage of time, acknowledged that their children would not always look like they looked now, secretly wished they wouldn't grow up, that they would always remain small enough to be held. They did not worry that these children would bleed to death on the floors of university classrooms. They did not imagine that their dying children would pretend to be dead in the hopes that they might stay alive.

Someday my son will ask about the shootings. Someday he will enter *Virginia* and *Tech* into a search engine, and it will automatically add *Massacre*. He will read the dates, do the math, realize he was alive and kicking not two miles away. He will have no memory of any of it, will not remember the time when his parents were glued to the television for hours on end, will have forgotten that his father became impatient when he clambered over him, how his father, when the shooter appeared on TV with his guns pointed at the audience, shielded his son's eyes.

*   *   *

Two years after the shootings, a Chinese student will remove a knife from a backpack and decapitate another Chinese student, a woman, in a place called the Graduate Life Center. He will walk around Au Bon Pain holding up her head.

The year after that, two students—a young man and a young woman—will be shot fatally at Caldwell Fields, a meadow skirted by a creek about twelve miles from campus. There will be no witnesses. There will be no suspects. The murderer will not be apprehended.

Four and a half years later, I will receive an email from VT Alerts that says "Gun shots reported—Coliseum Parking lot. Stay Inside. Secure doors. Emergency personnel responding. Call 911 for help." Despite the tone of the message—and despite the fact that I was on campus during the shootings on April 16, 2007—I shrug it off. Six months earlier, students at a Virginia Tech summer camp claimed they saw a man carrying a gun across campus. Nothing came of it. Furthermore, I am now accustomed to receiving emails from VT Alerts on a regular basis; they inform me of robberies and assaults—however few—that occur on Virginia Tech's campus.

So untroubled am I by reports of gunshots that I plan to go about my day, which involves driving to campus to meet a student in my office. But as I begin walking toward Shanks, having parked my car, I realize that nobody's out, anywhere. I slide out my phone and read an email from VT Alerts informing me: "A police officer has been shot. A potential second victim is reported at the Cage lot. Stay indoors. Secure in place."

I reach my building. It's locked. I take out my keys, open the door, but can't get the key back out. I twist and turn and tug. I panic a little. It's exactly like the movies when the main character is trying to get the car key into the ignition but can't, and there's no explanation for why this one simple thing that should work, doesn't. After maybe thirty seconds, I retrieve the keys, ascend the stairs to my floor. All doors closed. I feel safer in my office, where I load Twitter and CNN. *Déjà vu*, I think. I can't believe this is happening. Again. It's two hours before my department chair knocks on my door, tells me it's safe to leave. A day will pass before we learn that the assailant was a Radford University student, and that he'd shot the policeman and, minutes later, himself.

I tell myself I remain untroubled. I do not seek counseling. I am not plagued by fear or nightmares. But I often imagine dying. I ride my bike on the Huckleberry Trail, see guys dressed vaguely like thugs or gangbangers, imagine them unzipping hoodies to reveal bandoliers, cocking their Glocks and blasting holes through my torso. I pass people on campus who look weird or unkempt or simply just mean, and I imagine them sliding firearms from their waistbands, spraying my brains against Hokie stone. For me, violence is a sick reconstructed fantasy that I replay over and over, if only to prepare myself for the moment when it happens for real, and I can say, with some detachment, *This is exactly how I imagined it.*

There's a computer in the corner of the second floor of Virginia Tech's Newman library reserved especially for those who wish to read official documents pertaining to the events of April 16, 2007. I've considered visiting the terminal on a number of occasions, but the sign above the monitor, which announces that the computer is to be used only for accessing the special database, has acted as much as a deterrent as advertisement, and for years, I've been too sheepish to visit. I can't explain why, really, except maybe to say I had no "good" reason to do so, and worried that anyone who saw me sitting there—in front of a screen that faces a corner, so as to guarantee privacy for its user—would attribute my browsing to some kind of morbid curiosity. Perhaps this designation has prevented others from visiting as well; I've never seen anyone else accessing the database—that is, until today, when I decide to visit the library with the sole intent of accessing it myself. But the person—a bearded man with glasses—who's parked himself before the monitor is not performing research; he's an employee updating security software. When I return later to find the station vacant, I'm unable to access the database, in part because it requires a log in I don't have. I visit the information desk, summon a librarian. He leads me back to the terminal, rifles through a few handouts in a plastic holder, fails to find the instructions. I mention that I've never seen a soul using the computer. He's not surprised. He hasn't been asked by anybody for the log in in two years.

Five years have passed since the shootings and I still think about them almost every time I visit campus. This commemoration isn't willful; it's automatic. The green expanse of the Drill Field; the Burruss tower; the statues above War Memorial Chapel; the wooden doors of Norris Hall, which once fluttered with police tape; the sight of a bus pulling up to a stop and opening its doors: any and all of these everyday images have the power, at any time, to transport me to the events of April 16. That's why the phrase *Never Forget*—a phrase one still finds on T-shirts and magnets and bumper stickers—strikes me as absurd. I couldn't forget if I wanted to.

Eventually, though, people *will* forget. Or, to put it more accurately, they will fail to remember. Future students and visitors to the university—those who were shielded from the news footage, those who were too young to process it, and those who were born after the events of 4/16—will stand before the memorial stones on the Drill Field and read the names of the victims and recall nothing in particular. However horrifying, however inconceivable, the memories of this violence will dissolve with the bodies that carry them.

For now, though, those who hear about the infrequent bursts of violence on campus remember the day they heard about the thirty-three who died and feel compelled to offer us their condolences, express their disbelief. Some of them ask point blank if we're cursed. We, of all people, don't know. It's difficult to persuade others we aren't. We don't feel like we are. We live in a kind of paradise. In some ways, it is not so different from the world the Ingleses and other English settlers inhabited in the mid-eighteenth century, when they lived in Draper's Meadow. We have blue mountains and green hills. We see foxes under our overpasses; deer graze upon our lawns. The world's second-oldest river flows through our county. We know our neighbors and have genuine affection for them. We often leave our doors unlocked. Our children run through their yards, unsupervised, unimpeded, wild. We stand outside at night, under the stars, and despite all that has happened, and because it is something we are committed to feeling, we tell ourselves that we are safe, and that now the worst of it must be over.

Tom Wolfe

The Last American Hero is Junior Johnson.
Yes!

Ten o'clock Sunday morning in the hills of North Carolina. Cars, miles of cars, in every direction, millions of cars, pastel cars, aqua green, aqua blue, aqua beige, aqua buff, aqua dawn, aqua dusk, aqua aqua, aqua Malacca, Malacca lacquer, Cloud lavender, Assassin pink, Rake-a-cheek raspberry. Nude Strand coral, Honest Thrill orange, and Baby Fawn Lust cream-colored cars are all going to the stock-car races, and that old mothering North Carolina sun keeps exploding off the windshields. Mother dog!

Seventeen thousand people, me included, all of us driving out Route 421, out to the stock-car races at the North Wilkesboro Speedway, 17,000 going out to a five-eighths-mile stock-car track with a Coca-Cola sign out front. This is not to say there is no preaching and shouting in the South this morning. There is preaching and shouting. Any of us can turn on the old automobile transistor radio and get all we want:

"They are greedy dogs. Yeah! They ride around in big cars. Unnh-hunh! And chase women. Yeah! And drink liquor. Unnh-hunh! And smoke cigars. Oh yes! And they are greedy dogs. Yeah! Unnh-hunh! Oh yes! Amen!"

There are also some commercials on the radio for Aunt Jemima grits, which cost ten cents a pound. There are also the Gospel Harmonettes, singing: "If you dig a ditch, you better dig two. . . ."

There are also three fools in a panel discussion on the New South, which they seem to conceive of as General Lee running the new Dulcidreme Labial Cream factory down at Griffin, Georgia.

And suddenly my car is stopped still on Sunday morning in the middle of the biggest traffic jam in the history of the world. It goes for ten miles in every direction from the North Wilkesboro Speedway. And right there it dawns on me that as far as this situation is concerned, anyway, all the conventional notions about the South are confined to . . . the Sunday radio. The South has preaching and shouting, the South has grits, the South has country songs, old mimosa traditions, clay dust, Old Bigots, New Liberals—and all of it, all of that old mental cholesterol, is confined to the Sunday radio. What I was in the middle of—well, it wasn't anything one hears about in panels about the South today. Miles and miles of eye-busting pastel cars on the expressway, which roar right up into the hills, going to the stock-car races. In ten years baseball—and the state of North Carolina alone used to have forty-four professional baseball teams – baseball is all over with in the South. We are all in the middle of a wild new thing, the Southern car world, and heading down the road on my way to see a breed such as sports never saw before, Southern stock-car drivers, all lined up in these two-ton mothers that go over 175 m.p.h., Fireball Roberts, Freddie Lorenzen, Ned Jarrett, Richard Petty, and—the hardest of all the hard chargers, one of the fastest automobile racing drivers in history—yes! Junior Johnson.

The legend of Junior Johnson! In this legend, here is a country boy, Junior Johnson, who learns to drive by running whiskey for his father, Johnson, Senior, one of the biggest copper still operators of all times, up in Ingle Hollow, near North Wilkesboro, in northwestern North Carolina, and grows up to be a famous stock-car racing driver, rich, grossing $100,000 in 1963, for example, respected, solid, idolized in his hometown and throughout the rural South, for that matter. There is all this about how good old boys would wake up in the middle of the night in the apple shacks and hear an overcharged engine roaring over Brushy Mountain and say, "Listen at him—there he goes!", although that part is doubtful, since some nights there were so many good old boys taking off down the road in supercharged automobiles out of Wilkes County, and running loads to Charlotte, Salisbury, Greensboro, Winston-Salem, High Point, or wherever, it would be pretty hard to pick out one. It was Junior Johnson specifically, however, who was famous for the "bootleg turn" or "about-face," in which, if the Alcohol Tax agents had a roadblock up for you or were too close behind, you threw the car into second gear, cocked the wheel, stepped on the accelerator and made the car's rear end skid around in a complete 180-degree arc, a complete about-face, and tore on back up the road exactly the way you came from. God! The Alcohol Tax agents used to burn over Junior Johnson. Practically every good old boy in town in Wilkesboro, the county seat, got to know the agents by sight in a very short time. They would rag them practically to their faces on the subject of Junior Johnson, so that it got to be an obsession. Finally, one night they had Junior trapped on the road up toward the bridge around Millersville, there's no way out of there, they had the barricades up and they could hear this souped-up car roaring around the bend, and here it comes—but suddenly they can hear a siren and see a red light flashing in the grille, so they think it's another agent, and boy, they run out like ants and pull those barrels and boards and sawhorses out of the way, and then— Ggghhzzzzzzzhhhhhgggggggzzzzzzzeeeeeong!— gawdam! there he goes again, it was him, Junior Johnson!, with a gawdam agent's si-reen and a red light in his grille!

I wasn't in the South five minutes before people started making oaths, having visions, telling these hulking great stories, and so forth, all on the subject of Junior Johnson. At the Greensboro, North Carolina, Airport there was one good old boy who vowed he would have eaten "a bucket of it" if that would have kept Junior Johnson from switching from a Dodge racer to a Ford. Hell yes, and after that—God-almighty, remember that 1963 Chevrolet of Junior's? Whatever happened to that car? A couple of more good old boys join in. A good old boy, I ought to explain, is a generic term in the rural South referring to a man of any age, but more often young than not, who fits in with the status system of the region. It usually means he has a good sense of humor and enjoys ironic jokes, is tolerant and easygoing enough to get along in long conversations at places like on the corner, and has a reasonable amount of physical courage. The term is usually heard in some such form as: "Lud? He's a good old boy from over at Crozet." These good old boys in the airport, by the way, were in their twenties, except for one fellow who was a cabdriver and was about forty-five, I would say. Except for the cabdriver, they all wore neo-Brummellian wardrobe such as Lacoste tennis shirts, Slim Jim pants, windbreakers with the collars turned up, "fast" shoes of the winkle-picker genre, and so on. I mention these details just by way of pointing out that very few grits, Iron Boy overalls, clodhoppers or hats with ventilation holes up near the crown enter into this story. Anyway, these good old boys are talking about Junior Johnson and how he has switched to Ford. This they unanimously regard as some sort of betrayal on Johnson's part. Ford, it seems, they regard as the car symbolizing the established power structure. Dodge is a kind of middle ground. Dodge is at least a challenger, not a ruler. But the Junior Johnson they like to remember is the Junior Johnson of 1963, who took on the whole field of NASCAR (National Association for Stock Car Auto Racing) Grand National racing with a Chevrolet. All the other drivers, the drivers driving Fords, Mercurys, Plymouths, Dodges, had millions, literally millions when it is all added up, millions of dollars in backing from the Ford and Chrysler Corporations. Junior Johnson took them all on in a Chevrolet without one cent of backing from Detroit. Chevrolet had pulled out of stock-car racing. Yet every race it was the same. It was never a question of whether anybody was going to *outrun* Junior Johnson. It was just a question of whether he was going to win or his car was going to break down, since, for one thing, half the time he had to make his own racing parts. God! Junior Johnson was like Robin Hood or Jesse James or Little David or something. Every time that Chevrolet, No. 3, appeared on the track, wild curdled yells, "Rebel" yells, they still have those, would rise up. At Daytona, at Atlanta, at Charlotte, at Darlington, South Carolina; Bristol, Tennessee; Martinsville, Virginia—Junior Johnson!

And then the good old boys get to talking about whatever happened to that Chevrolet of Junior's, and the cabdriver says he knows. He says Junior Johnson is using that car to run liquor out of Wilkes County. What does he mean? For Junior Johnson ever to go near another load of bootleg whiskey again—he would have to be insane. He has this huge racing income. He has two other businesses, a whole automated chicken farm with 42,000 chickens, a road-grading business—but the cabdriver says he has this dream Junior is still roaring down from Wilkes County, down through the clay cuts, with the Atlas Arc Lip jars full in the back of that Chevrolet. It is in Junior's blood—and then at this point he puts his right hand up in front of him as if he is groping through fog, and his eyeballs glaze over and he looks out in the distance and he describes Junior Johnson roaring over the ridges of Wilkes County as if it is the ghost of Zapata he is describing, bounding over the Sierras on a white horse to rouse the peasants.

A stubborn notion! A crazy notion! Yet Junior Johnson has followers who need to keep him, symbolically, riding through nighttime like a demon. Madness! But Junior Johnson is one of the last of those sports stars who is not just an ace at the game itself, but a hero a whole people or class of people can identify with. Other, older examples are the way Jack Dempsey stirred up the Irish or the way Joe Louis stirred up the Negroes. Junior Johnson is a modern figure. He is only thirty-three years old and still racing. He should be compared to two other sports heroes whose cultural impact is not too well known. One is Antonino Rocca, the professional wrestler, whose triumphs mean so much to New York City's Puerto Ricans that he can fill Madison Square Garden, despite the fact that everybody, the Puerto Ricans included, knows that wrestling is nothing but a crude form of folk theatre. The other is Ingemar Johansson, who had a tremendous meaning to the Swedish masses—they were tired of that old king who played tennis all the time and all his friends who keep on drinking Cointreau behind the screen of socialism. Junior Johnson is a modern hero, all involved with car culture and car symbolism in the South. A wild new thing—

Wild—gone wild. Fireball Roberts' Ford spins out on the first turn at the North Wilkesboro Speedway, spinning, spinning, the spin seems almost like slow motion—and then it smashes into the wooden guardrail. It lies up there with the frame bent. Roberts is all right. There is a new layer of asphalt on the track, it is like glass, the cars keep spinning off the first turn. Ned Jarrett spins, smashes through the wood. "Now, boys, this ice ain't gonna get one goddamn bit better, so you can either line up and qualify or pack up and go home—"

I had driven from the Greensboro Airport up to Wilkes County to see Junior Johnson on the occasion of one of the two yearly NASCAR Grand National stock-car races at the North Wilkesboro Speedway.

It is a long, very gradual climb from Greensboro to Wilkes County. Wilkes County is all hills, ridges, woods and underbrush, full of pin oaks, sweetgum maples, ash, birch, apple trees, rhododendron, rocks, vines, tin roofs, little clapboard places like the Mount Olive Baptist Church, signs for things like Double Cola, Sherrill's Ice Cream, Eckard's Grocery, Dr. Pepper, Diel's Apples, Google's Place, Suddith's Place and—yes!—cars. Up onto the highway, out of a side road from a hollow, here comes a 1947 Hudson. To almost anybody it would look like just some old piece of junk left over from God knows when, rolling down a country road . . . the 1947 Hudson was one of the first real "hot" cars made after the war. Some of the others were the 1946 Chrysler, which had a "kick-down" gear for sudden bursts of speed, the 1955 Pontiac and a lot of the Fords. To a great many good old boys a hot car was a symbol of heating up life itself. The war! Money even for country boys! And the money bought cars. In California they suddenly found kids of all sorts involved in vast drag racing orgies and couldn't figure out what was going on. But in the South the mania for cars was even more intense, although much less publicized. To millions of good old boys, and girls, the automobile represented not only liberation from what was still pretty much a land-bound form of social organization but also a great leap forward into twentieth-century glamour, an idea that was being dinned on in the South like everywhere else. It got so that one of the typical rural sights, in addition to the red rooster, the gray split-rail fence, the Edgeworth Tobacco sign, and the rusted-out harrow, one of the typical rural sights would be . . . you would be driving along the dirt roads and there beside the house would be an automobile up on blocks or something, with a rope over the tree for hoisting up the motor or some other heavy part, and a couple of good old boys would be practically disappearing into its innards, from below and from above, draped over the side under the hood. It got so that on Sundays there wouldn't be a safe straight stretch of road in the county, because so many wild country boys would be out racing or just raising hell on the roads. A lot of other kids, who weren't basically wild, would be driving like hell every morning and every night, driving to jobs perhaps thirty or forty miles away, jobs that were available only because of automobiles. In the morning they would be driving through the dapple shadows like madmen. In the hollows, sometimes one would come upon the most incredible tar-paper hovels, down near the stream, and out front would be an incredible automobile creation, a late-model car with aerials, continental kit overhangs in the back, mudguards studded with reflectors, fender skirts, spotlights, God knows what all, with a girl and perhaps a couple of good old boys communing over it and giving you rotten looks as you drive by. On Saturday night everybody would drive into town and park under the lights on the main street and neck. Yes! There was something about being right in there in town underneath the lights and having them reflecting off the baked enamel on the hood. Then if a good old boy insinuated his hands here and there on the front seat with a girl and began . . . necking . . . somehow it was all more *complete*. After the war there was a great deal of stout-burgher talk about people who lived in hovels and bought big-yacht cars to park out front. This was one of the symbols of a new, spendthrift age. But there was a great deal of unconscious resentment buried in the talk. It was resentment against (a) the fact that the good old boy had his money at all and (b) the fact that the car symbolized freedom, a slightly wild, careening emancipation from the old social order. Stock-car racing got started about this time, right after the war, and it was immediately regarded as some kind of manifestation of the animal irresponsibility of the lower orders. It had a truly terrible reputation. It was—well, it looked *rowdy* or something. The cars were likely to be used cars, the tracks were dirt, the stands were rickety wood, the drivers were country boys, and they had regular feuds out there, putting each other "up against the wall" and "cutting tires" and everything else. Those country boys would drive into the curves full tilt, then slide maniacally, sometimes coming around the curve sideways, with red dirt showering up. Sometimes they would race at night, under those weak-eyed yellow-ochre lights they have at small tracks and baseball fields, and the clay dust would start showering up in the air, where the evening dew would catch it, and all evening long you would be sitting in the stands or standing out in the infield with a fine clay-mud drizzle coming down on you, not that anybody gave a damn—except for the Southern upper and middle classes, who never attended in those days but spoke of the "rowdiness."

But mainly it was the fact that stock-car racing was something that was welling up out of the lower orders. From somewhere these country boys and urban proles were getting the money and starting this sport.

Stock-car racing was beginning all over the country, at places like Allentown, Langhorne, and Lancaster, Pennsylvania, and out in California and even out on Long Island, but wherever it cropped up, the Establishment tried to wish it away, largely, and stock-car racing went on in a kind of underground world of tracks built on cheap stretches of land well out from the town or the city, a world of diners, drive-ins, motels, gasoline stations, and the good burghers might drive by from time to time, happen by on a Sunday or something, and see the crowd gathered from out of nowhere, the cars coming in, crowding up the highway a little, but Monday morning they would be all gone.

Stock-car racing was building up a terrific following in the South during the early Fifties. Here was a sport not using any abstract devices, any *bat* and *ball*, but the same automobile that was changing a man's own life, his own symbol of liberation, and it didn't require size, strength and all that, all it required was a taste for speed, and the guts. The newspapers in the South didn't seem to catch on to what was happening until late in the game. Of course, newspapers all over the country have looked backward over the tremendous rise in automobile sports, now the second-biggest type of sport in the country in terms of attendance. The sports pages generally have an inexorable lower-middle-class outlook. The sportswriter's "zest for life" usually amounts, in the end, to some sort of gruff Mom's Pie sentimentality at a hideously cozy bar somewhere. The sportswriters caught on to Grand Prix racing first because it had "tone," a touch of defrocked European nobility about it, what with a few counts racing here and there, although, in fact, it is the least popular form of racing in the United States. What finally put stock-car racing onto the sports pages in the South was the intervention of the Detroit automobile firms. Detroit began putting so much money into the sport that it took on a kind of massive economic respectability and thereby, in the lower-middle-class brain, status.

What Detroit discovered was that thousands of good old boys in the South were starting to form allegiances to brands of automobiles, according to which were hottest on the stock-car circuits, the way they used to have them for the hometown baseball team. The South was one of the hottest car-buying areas in the country. Cars like Hudsons, Oldsmobiles, and Lincolns, not the cheapest automobiles by any means, were selling in disproportionate numbers in the South, and a lot of young good old boys were buying them. In 1955, Pontiac started easing into stock-car racing, and suddenly the big surge was on. Everybody jumped into the sport to grab for themselves The Speed Image. Suddenly, where a good old boy used to have to bring his gasoline to the track in old filling-station pails and pour it into the tank through a funnel when he made a pit stop, and change his tires with a hand wrench, suddenly, now, he had these "gravity" tanks of gasoline that you just jam into the gas pipe, and air wrenches to take the wheels off, and whole crews of men in white coveralls to leap all over a car when it came rolling into the pit, just like they do at Indianapolis, as if they are mechanical apparati *merging* with the machine as it rolls in, forcing water into the radiator, jacking up the car, taking off wheels, wiping off the windshield, handing the driver a cup of orange juice, all in one synchronized operation. And now, today, the *big money* starts descending on this little place, the North Wilkesboro, North Carolina, Speedway, a little five-eighths-of-a-mile stock-car track with a Coca-Cola sign out by the highway where the road in starts.

The private planes start landing out at the Wilkesboro Airport. Freddie Lorenzen, the driver, the biggest money winner last year in stock-car racing, comes sailing in out of the sky in a twin-engine Aero Commander, and there are a few good old boys out there in the tall grass by the runway already with their heads sticking up watching this hero of the modern age come in and taxi up and get out of that twin-engine airplane with his blond hair swept back as if by the mother internal combustion engine of them all. And then Paul Goldsmith, the driver, comes in in a 310 Cessna, and *he* gets out, all these tall, lanky hard-boned Americans in their thirties with these great profiles like a comic-strip hero or something, and then Glenn (Fireball) Roberts—Fireball Roberts!—Fireball is *hard*—he comes in a Comanche 250, like a flying yacht, and then Ray Nichels and Ray Fox, the chief mechanics, who run big racing crews for the Chrysler Corporation, this being Fox's last race for Junior as his mechanic, before Junior switches over to Ford, they come in in two-engine planes. And even old Buck Baker—hell, Buck Baker is a middling driver for Dodge, but even he comes rolling in down the landing strip at two hundred miles an hour with his Southern-hero face at the window of the cockpit of a twin-engine Apache, traveling first class in the big status boat that has replaced the yacht in America, the private plane.

And then the Firestone and Goodyear vans pull in, huge mothers, bringing in huge stacks of racing tires for the race, big wide ones, 8.20s, with special treads, which are like a lot of bumps on the tire instead of grooves. They even have special tires for qualifying, soft tires, called "gumballs," they wouldn't last more than ten times around the track in a race, but for qualifying, which is generally three laps, one to pick up speed and two to race against the clock, they are great, because they hold tight on the comers. And on a hot day, when somebody like Junior Johnson, one of the fastest qualifying runners in the history of the sport, 170.777 m.p.h. in a one-hundred-mile qualifying race at Daytona in 1964, when somebody like Junior Johnson really pushes it on a qualifying run, there will be a ring of blue smoke up over the whole goddamned track, a ring like an oval halo over the whole thing from the gumballs burning, and some good old boy will say, "Great smokin' blue gumballs god almighty dog! There goes Junior Johnson!"

The thing is, each one of these tires costs fifty-five to sixty dollars, and on a track that is fast and hard on tires, like Atlanta, one car might go through ten complete tire changes, easily, forty tires, or almost $2500 worth of tires just for one race. And he may even be out of the money. And then the Ford van and the Dodge van and the Mercury van and the Plymouth van roll in with new motors, a whole new motor every few races, a 427-cubic-inch stock-car racing motor, 600 horsepower, the largest and most powerful allowed on the track, that probably costs the company $1000 or more, when you consider that they are not mass produced. And still the advertising appeal. You can buy the very same car that these fabulous wild men drive every week at these fabulous wild speeds, and some of their power and charisma is yours. After every NASCAR Grand National stock-car race, whichever company has the car that wins, this company will put big ads in the Southern papers, and papers all over the country if it is a very big race, like the Daytona 500, the Daytona Firecracker 400, or the Atlanta and Charlotte races. They sell a certain number of these 427-cubic-inch cars to the general public, a couple of hundred a year, perhaps, at eight or nine thousand dollars apiece, but it is no secret that these motors are specially reworked just for stock-car racing. Down at Charlotte there is a company called Holman & Moody that is supposed to be the "garage" or "automotive-engineering" concern that prepares automobiles for Freddy Lorenzen and some of the other Ford drivers. But if you go by Holman & Moody out by the airport and Charlotte, suddenly you come upon a huge place that is a *factory*, for God's sake, a big long thing, devoted mainly to the business of turning out stock-car racers. A whole lot of other parts in stock-car racers are heavier than the same parts on a street automobile, although they are made to the same scale. The shock absorbers are bigger, the wheels are wider and bulkier, the swaybars and steering mechanisms are heavier, the axles are much heavier, they have double sets of wheel bearings, and so forth and so on. The bodies of the cars are pretty much the same, except that they use lighter sheet metal, practically tinfoil. Inside, there is only the driver's seat and a heavy set of roll bars and diagonal struts that turn the inside of the car into a rigid cage, actually. That is why the drivers can walk away unhurt—most of the time—from the most spectacular crackups. The gearshift is the floor kind, although it doesn't make much difference, as there is almost no shifting gears in stock-car racing. You just get into high gear and go. The dashboard has no speedometer, the main thing being the dial for engine revolutions per minute. So, anyway, it costs about $15,000 to prepare a stock-car racer in the first place and another three or four thousand for each new race and this does not even count the costs of mechanics' work and transportation. All in all, Detroit will throw around a quarter of a million dollars into it every week while the season is on, and the season runs, roughly, from February to October, with a few big races after that. And all this turns up even out at the North Wilkesboro Speedway with the Coca-Cola sign out front, out in the up-country of Wilkes County, North Carolina.

Sunday! Racing day! Sunday is no longer a big church day in the South. A man can't very well go to eleven o'clock service and still expect to get to a two o'clock stock-car race, unless he wants to get into the biggest traffic jam in the history of creation, and that goes for North Wilkesboro, North Carolina, same as Atlanta and Charlotte.

There is the Coca-Cola sign out where the road leads in from the highway, and hills and trees, but here are long concrete grandstands for about 17,000 and a paved five-eighths-mile oval. Practically all the drivers are out there with their cars and their crews, a lot of guys in white coveralls. The cars look huge . . . and curiously nude and blind. All the chrome is stripped off, except for the grilles. The headlights are blanked out. Most of the cars are in the pits. The so-called "pit" is a paved cutoff on the edge of the infield. It cuts off from the track itself like a service road off an expressway at the shopping center. Every now and then a car splutters, hacks, coughs, hocks a lunga, rumbles out onto the track itself for a practice run. There is a lot of esoteric conversation going on, speculation, worries, memoirs:

"What happened?"

"Mother—condensed on me. Al brought it up here with him. Water in the line."

"Better keep Al away from a stable, he'll fill you up with horse manure."

". . . they told me to give him one, a cream puff, so I give him one, a cream puff. One goddamn race and the son of a bitch, he *melted* it. . . ."

". . . he's down there right now pettin' and rubbin' and huggin' that car just like those guys do a horse at the Kentucky Derby. . . ."

". . . They'll blow you right out of the tub. . . ."

". . . No, the quarter inch, and go on over and see if you can get Ned's blowtorch. . . ."

". . . Rear end's loose. . . ."

". . . I don't reckon this right here's got nothing to do with it, do you? . . ."

". . . Aw, I don't know, about yay big. . . ."

". . . Who the hell stacked them gumballs on the bottom? . . ."

". . . th'ow in rocks. . . ."

". . . won't turn seven thousand. . . ."

". . . strokin' it. . . ."

". . . blistered. . . ."

". . . spun out. . . ."

". . . muvva. . . ."

Then, finally, here comes Junior Johnson. How he does come on. He comes tooling across the infield in a big white dreamboat, a brand-new white Pontiac Catalina four-door hard-top sedan. He pulls up and as he gets out he seems to get more and more huge. First his crew-cut head and then a big jaw and then a bigger neck and then a huge torso, like a wrestler's, all done up rather modish and California modern, with a red-and-white candy-striped sport shirt, white ducks and loafers.

"How you doing?" says Junior Johnson, shaking hands, and then he says, "Hot enough for ye'uns?" Junior is in an amiable mood. Like most up-hollow people, it turns out, Junior is reserved. His face seldom shows an emotion. He has three basic looks: amiable, amiable and a little shy, and dead serious. To a lot of people, apparently, Junior's dead-serious look seems menacing. There are no cowards left in stock-car racing, but a couple of drivers tell me that one of the things that can shake you up is to look into your rearview mirror going around a curve and see Junior Johnson's car on your tail trying to "root you out of the groove," and then get a glimpse of Junior's dead-serious look. I think some of the sportswriters are afraid of him. One of them tells me Junior is strong, silent—and explosive. Junior will only give you three answers, "Uh-huh," "Uh-unh," and "I don't know," and so forth and so on. Actually, I find he handles questions easily. He has a great technical knowledge of automobiles and the physics of speed, including things he never fools with, such as Offenhauser engines. What he never does offer, however, is small talk. This gives him a built-in poise, since it deprives him of the chance to say anything asinine. "Ye'uns," "we'uns," "h'it" for "it," "growed" for "grew," and a lot of other unusual past participles— Junior uses certain older forms of English, not exactly "Elizabethan," as they are sometimes called, but older forms of English preserved up-country in his territory, Ingle Hollow.

Kids keep coming up for Junior's autograph and others are just hanging around and one little old boy comes up, he is about thirteen, and Junior says: "This boy here goes coon hunting with me."

One of the sportswriters is standing around, saying: "What do you shoot a coon with?"

"Don't shoot 'em. The dogs tree 'em and then you flush 'em out and the dogs fight 'em."

"Flush 'em out?"

"Yeah. This boy right here can flush 'em out better than anybody you ever did see. You go out at night with the dogs, and soon as they get the scent, they start barking. They go on out ahead of you and when they tree a coon, you can tell it, by the way they sound. They all start baying up at that coon—h'it sounds like, I don't know, you hear it once and you not likely to forget it. Then you send a little old boy up to flush him out and he jumps down and the dogs fight him."

"How does a boy flush him out?"

"Aw, he just climbs up there to the limb he's on and starts shaking h'it and the coon'll jump."

"What happens if the coon decides he'd rather come back after the boy instead of jumping down to a bunch of dogs?"

"He won't do that. A coon's afraid of a person, but he can kill a dog. A coon can take any dog you set against him if they's just the two of them fighting. The coon jumps down on the ground and he rolls right over on his back with his feet up, and he's *got* claws about like this. All he has to do is get a dog once in the throat or in the belly, and he can kill him, cut him wide open just like you took a knife and did it. Won't any dog even fight a coon except a coon dog."

"What kind of dogs are they?"

"*Coon* dogs, I guess. Black and tans they call 'em sometimes. They's bred for it. If his mammy and pappy wasn't coon dogs, he ain't likely to be one either. After you got one, you got to train him. You trap a coon, live, and then you put him in a pen and tie him to a post with a rope on him and then you put your dog in there and he has to fight him. Sometimes you get a dog just don't have any fight in him and he ain't no good to you."

Junior is in the pit area, standing around with his brother Fred, who is part of his crew, and Ray Fox and some other good old boys, in a general atmosphere of big stock-car money, a big ramp truck for his car, a white Dodge, number 3, a big crew in white coveralls, huge stacks of racing tires, a Dodge P.R. man, big portable cans of gasoline, compressed air hoses, compressed water hoses, the whole business. Herb Nab, Freddie Lorenzen's chief mechanic, comes over and sits down on his haunches and Junior sits down on his haunches and Nab says:

"So Junior Johnson's going to drive a Ford."

Junior is switching from Dodge to Ford mainly because he hasn't been winning with the Dodge. Lorenzen drives a Ford, too, and the last year, when Junior was driving the Chevrolet, their duels were the biggest excitement in stock-car racing.

"Well," says Nab, "I'll tell you, Junior. My ambition is going to be to outrun your ass every goddamned time we go out."

"That was your ambition last year," says Junior.

"I know it was," says Nab, "and you took all the money, didn't you? You know what my strategy was. I was going to outrun everybody else and outlast Junior, that was my strategy."

Setting off his California modern sport shirt and white ducks Junior has on a pair of twenty-dollar rimless sunglasses and a big gold Timex watch, and Flossie, his fiancée, is out there in the infield somewhere with the white Pontiac, and the white Dodge that Dodge gave Junior is parked up near the pit area—and then a little thing happens that brings the whole thing right back there to Wilkes County, North Carolina, to Ingle Hollow and to hard muscle in the clay gulches. A couple of good old boys come down to the front of the stands with the screen and the width of the track between them and Junior, and one of the good old boys comes down and yells out in the age-old baritone raw curdle yell of the Southern hills:

"Hey, hog jaw!"

Everybody gets quiet. They know he's yelling at Junior, but nobody says a thing. Junior doesn't even turn around.

"Hey, hog jaw! . . ."

Junior, he does nothing.

"Hey, hog jaw, I'm gonna get me one of them fastback roosters, too, and come down there and get you!"

Fastback rooster refers to the Ford—it has a "fastback" design—Junior is switching to.

"Hey, hog jaw, I'm gonna get me one of them fastback roosters and run you right out of here, you hear me, hog jaw!"

One of the good old boys alongside Junior says, "Junior, go on up there and clear out those stands."

Then everybody stares at Junior to see what he's gonna do. Junior, he don't even look around. He just looks a bit dead serious.

"Hey, hog jaw, you got six cases of whiskey in the back of that car you want to let me have?"

"What you hauling in that car, hog jaw!"

"Tell him you're out of that business, Junior," one of the good old boys says.

"Go on up there and clean house, Junior," says another good old boy.

Then Junior looks up, without looking at the stands and smiles a little and says, "You fish him down here out of that tree—and I'll take keer of him."

Such a howl goes up from the good old boys! It is almost a blood curdle—

"Goddamn, he *will*, too!"

"Lord, he better know how to do an *about-face* hisself if he comes down here!"

"Goddamn, get him, Junior!"

"Whooeeee!"

"Mother dog!"

A kind of orgy of reminiscence of the old Junior before the Detroit money started flowing, wild combats *d'honneur* up-hollow—and, suddenly, when he heard that unearthly baying coming up from the good old boys in the pits, the good old boy retreated from the edge of the stands and never came back.

Later on Junior told me, sort of apologetically, "H'it used to be, if a fellow crowded me just a little bit, I was ready to crawl him. I reckon that was one good thing about Chillicothe.

"I don't want to pull any more time," Junior tells me, "but I wouldn't take anything in the world for the experience I had in prison. If a man needed to change, that was the place to change. H'it's not a waste of time there, h'it's good experience.

"H'it's that they's so many people in the world

that feel that nobody is going to tell them what to do. I had quite a temper, I reckon. I always had the idea that I had as much sense as the other person and I didn't want them to tell me what to do. In the penitentiary there I found out that I could listen to another fellow and be told what to do and h'it wouldn't kill me."

Starting time! Linda Vaughn, with the big blonde hair and blossomy breasts, puts down her Coca-Cola and the potato chips and slips off her red stretch pants and her white blouse and walks out of the officials' booth in her Rake-a-cheek red showgirl's costume with her long honeydew legs in net stockings and climbs up on the red Firebird float. The Life Symbol of stock-car racing! Yes! Linda, every luscious morsel of Linda, is a good old girl from Atlanta who was made Miss Atlanta International Raceway one year and was paraded around the track on a float and she liked it so much and all the good old boys liked it so much, Linda's flowing hair and blossomy breasts and honeydew legs, that she became the permanent glamour symbol of stock-car racing, and never mind this other modeling she was doing . . . this, she liked it. Right before practically every race on the Grand National circuit Linda Vaughn puts down her Coca-Cola and potato chips. Her momma is there, she generally comes around to see Linda go around the track on the float, it's such a nice spectacle seeing Linda looking so lovely, and the applause and all. "Linda, I'm thirstin', would you bring me a Coca-Cola?" "A lot of them think I'm Freddie Lorenzen's girlfriend, but I'm not any of 'em's girlfriend, I'm real good friends with 'em all, even Wendell," he being Wendell Scott, the only Negro in big-league stock-car racing. Linda gets up on the Firebird float. This is an extraordinary object, made of wood, about twenty feet tall, in the shape of a huge bird, an eagle or something, blazing red, and Linda, with her red showgirl's suit on, gets up on the seat, which is up between the wings, like a saddle, high enough so her long honeydew legs stretch down, and a new car pulls her—Miss Firebird!—slowly once around the track just before the race. It is more of a ceremony by now than the national anthem. Miss Firebird sails slowly in front of the stands and the good old boys let out some real curdle Rebel yells, "Yaaaaaaaaaaaaghhhhoooooo! Let me at that car!" "Honey, you sure do start my motor, I swear to God!" "Great God and Poonadingdong, I mean!"

And suddenly there's a big roar from behind, down in the infield, and then I see one of the great sights in stock-car racing. That infield! The cars have been piling into the infield by the hundreds, parking in there on the clay and the grass, every which way, angled down and angled up, this way and that, where the ground is uneven, these beautiful blazing brand-new cars with the sun exploding off the windshields and the baked enamel and the glassy lacquer, hundreds, thousands of cars stacked this way and that in the infield with the sun bolting down and no shade, none at all, just a couple of Coca-Cola stands out there. And already the good old boys and girls are out beside the cars, with all these beautiful little buds in short shorts already spread-eagled out on top of the car roofs, pressing down on good hard slick automobile sheet metal, their little cupcake bottoms aimed up at the sun. The good old boys are lollygagging around with their shirts off and straw hats on that have miniature beer cans on the brims and buttons that read, "Girls Wanted—No Experience Required." And everybody, good old boys and girls of all ages, are out there with portable charcoal barbecue ovens set up, and folding tubular steel terrace furniture, deck chairs and things, and Thermos jugs and coolers full of beer—and suddenly it is not the up-country South at all but a concentration of the modern suburbs, all jammed into that one space, from all over America, with blazing cars and instant goodies, all cooking under the bare blaze—inside a strange bowl. The infield is like the bottom of a bowl. The track around it is banked so steeply at the corners and even on the straightaways, it is like . . . the steep sides of a bowl. The wall around the track, and the stands and the bleachers are like . . . the rim of a bowl. And from the infield, in this great incredible press of blazing new cars, there is no horizon but the bowl, up above only that cobalt-blue North Carolina sky. And then suddenly, on a signal, thirty stock-car engines start up where they are lined up in front of the stands. The roar of these engines is impossible to describe. They have a simultaneous rasp, thunder, and rumble that goes right through a body and fills the whole bowl with a noise of internal combustion. Then they start around on two build-up runs, just to build up speed, and then they come around the fourth turn and onto the straightaway in front of the stands at— here, 130 miles an hour, in Atlanta, 160 miles an hour, at Daytona, 180 miles an hour—and the flag goes down and everybody in the infield and in the stands is up on their feet going mad, and suddenly here is a bowl that is one great orgy of everything in the way of excitement and liberation the automobile has meant to Americans. An orgy!

The first lap of a stock-car race is a horrendous, a wildly horrendous spectacle such as no other sport approaches. Twenty, thirty, forty automobiles, each of them weighing almost two tons, 3700 pounds, with 427-cubic-inch engines, 600 horsepower, are practically locked together, side to side and tail to nose, on a narrow band of asphalt at 130, 160, 180 miles an hour, hitting the curves so hard the rubber burns off the tires in front of your eyes. To the driver, it is like being inside a car going down the West Side Highway in New York City at rush hour, only with everybody going literally three to four times as fast, at speeds a man who has gone eighty-five miles an hour down a highway cannot conceive of, and with every other driver an enemy who is willing to cut inside of you, around you or in front of you, or ricochet off your side in the battle to get into a curve first.

The speeds are faster than those in the Indianapolis 500 race, the cars are more powerful and much heavier, and the drivers have more courage, more daring, more ruthlessness than Indianapolis or Grand Prix drivers. The prize money in Southern stock-car racing is far greater than that in Indianapolis-style or European Grand Prix racing, but few Indianapolis or Grand Prix drivers have the raw nerve required to succeed at it.

Although they will deny it, it is still true that stock-car drivers will put each other "up against the wall"—cut inside on the left of another car and ram it into a spin—if they get mad enough. Crashes are not the only danger, however. The cars are now literally too fast for their own parts, especially the tires. Firestone and Goodyear have poured millions into stock-car racing, but neither they nor anybody else so far have been able to come up with a tire for this kind of racing at the current speeds. Three well-known stock-car drivers were killed last year, two of them champion drivers, Joe Weatherly and Fireball Roberts, and another, one of the best new drivers, Jimmy Pardue, from Junior Johnson's own home territory, Wilkes County, North Carolina. Roberts was the only one killed in a crash. Junior Johnson was in the crash but was not injured. Weatherly and Pardue both lost control on curves. Pardue's death came during a tire test. In a tire test, engineers, from Firestone or Goodyear, try out various tires on a car, and the driver, always one of the top competitors, tests them at top speed, usually on the Atlanta track. The drivers are paid three dollars a mile and may drive as much as five or six hundred miles in a single day. At 145 miles an hour average that does not take very long. Anyway, these drivers are going at speeds that, on curves, can tear tires off their casings or break axles. They practically run off from over their own automobiles.

Junior Johnson was over in the garden by the house some years ago, plowing the garden barefooted, behind a mule, just wearing an old pair of overalls, when a couple of good old boys drove up and told him to come on up to the speedway and get in a stock-car race. They wanted some local boys to race, as a preliminary to the main race, "as a kind of side show," as Junior remembers it.

"So I just put the reins down," Junior is telling

me, "and rode on over 'ere with them. They didn't give us seat belts or nothing, they just roped us in. H'it was a dirt track then. I come in second."

Junior was a sensation in dirt-track racing right from the start. Instead of going into the curves and just sliding and holding on for dear life like the other drivers, Junior developed the technique of throwing himself into a slide about seventy-five feet before the curve by cocking the wheel to the left slightly and gunning it, using the slide, not the brake, to slow down, so that he could pick up speed again halfway through the curve and come out of it like a shot. This was known as his "power slide," and—yes! of course!—every good old boy in North Carolina started saying Junior Johnson had learned that stunt doing those goddamned *about-faces* running away from the Alcohol Tax agents. Junior put on such a show one night on a dirt track in Charlotte that he broke two axles, and he thought he was out of the race because he didn't have any more axles, when a good old boy came running up out of the infield and said, "Goddamn it, Junior Johnson, you take the axle off my car here, I got a Pontiac just like yours," and Junior took it off and put it on his and went out and broke *it* too. Mother dog! To this day Junior Johnson loves dirt-track racing like nothing else in this world, even though there is not much money in it. Every year he sets new dirt-track speed records, such as at Hickory, North Carolina, one of the most popular dirt tracks, last spring. As far as Junior is concerned, dirt-track racing is not so much of a mechanical test for the car as those long five- and six-hundred-mile races on asphalt are. Gasoline, tire, and engine wear aren't so much of a problem. It is all the driver, his skill, his courage—his willingness to mix it up with the other cars, smash and carom off of them at a hundred miles an hour or so to get into the curves first. Junior has a lot of fond recollections of mixing it up at places like Bowman Gray Stadium in Winston-Salem, one of the minor league tracks, a very narrow track, hardly wide enough for two cars. "You could always figure Bowman Gray was gonna cost you two fenders, two doors, and two quarter panels," Junior tells me with nostalgia.

Anyway, at Hickory, which was a Saturday night race, all the good old boys started pouring into the stands before sundown, so they wouldn't miss anything, the practice runs or the qualifying or anything. And pretty soon, the dew hasn't even started falling before Junior Johnson and David Pearson, one of Dodge's best drivers, are out there on practice runs, just warming up, and they happen to come up alongside each other on the second curve, and—the thing is, here are two men, each of them driving $15,000 automobiles, each of them standing to make $50,000 to $100,000 for the season if they don't get themselves killed, and they meet on a curve on a goddamned practice run on a dirt track, and neither of them can resist it. Coming out of the turn they go into a wild-ass race down the backstretch, both of them trying to get into the third turn first, and all the way across the infield you can hear them ricocheting off each other and bouncing at a hundred miles an hour on loose dirt, and then they go into ferocious power slides, red dust all over the goddamned place, and then out of this goddamned red-dust cloud, out of the fourth turn, here comes Junior Johnson first, like a shot, with Pearson right on his tail, and the good old boys in the stands going wild, and the *qualifying* runs haven't started yet, let alone the race.

Junior worked his way up through the minor leagues, the Sportsman and Modified classifications, as they are called, winning championships in both, and won his first Grand National race, the big leagues, in 1955 at Hickory, on dirt. He was becoming known as "the hardest of the hard-chargers," power sliding, rooting them out of the groove, raising hell, and already the Junior Johnson legend was beginning.

He kept hard-charging, power sliding, going after other drivers as though there wasn't room on the track but for one, and became the most popular driver in stock-car racing by 1959. The automobile companies had suddenly dropped out of stock-car racing in 1957, making a devout covenant never again to capitalize on speed as a selling point, the Government was getting stuffy about it, but already the presence of Detroit and Detroit's big money had begun to calm the drivers down a little. Detroit was concerned about Image. The last great duel of the dying dog-eat-dog era of stock-car racing came in 1959, when Junior and Lee Petty, who was then leading the league in points, had it out on the Charlotte raceway. Junior was in the lead, and Petty was right on his tail, but couldn't get by Junior. Junior kept coming out of the curves faster. So every chance he got, Petty would get up right on Junior's rear bumper and start banging it, gradually forcing the fender in to where the metal would cut Junior's rear tire. With only a few laps to go, Junior had a blowout and spun out up against the guardrail. That is Junior's version. Petty claimed Junior hit a pop bottle and spun out. The fans in Charlotte were always throwing pop bottles and other stuff onto the track late in the race, looking for blood. In any case, Junior eased back into the pits, had the tire changed, and charged out after Petty. He caught him on a curve and—well, whatever really happened, Petty was suddenly "up against the wall" and out of the race, and Junior won.

What a howl went up. The Charlotte chief of police charged out onto the track after the race, according to Petty, and offered to have Junior arrested for "assault with a dangerous weapon," the hassling went on for weeks—

"Back then," Junior tells me, "when you got into a guy and racked him up, you might as well get ready, because he's coming back for you. H'it was dog eat dog. That straightened Lee Petty out right smart. They don't do stuff like that anymore, though, because the guys don't stand for it."

Anyway, the Junior Johnson legend kept building up and building up, and in 1960 it got better than ever when Junior won the biggest race of the year, the Daytona 500, by "discovering" a new technique called "drafting." That year stock-car racing was full of big powerful Pontiacs manned by top drivers, and they would go like nothing else anybody ever saw. Junior went down to Daytona with a Chevrolet.

"My car was about ten miles an hour slower than the rest of the cars, the Pontiacs," Junior tells me. "In the preliminary races, the warmups and stuff like that, they was smoking me off the track. Then I remember once I went out for a practice run, and Fireball Roberts was out there in a Pontiac and I got in right behind him on a curve, right on his bumper. I knew I couldn't stay with him on the straightaway, but I came out of the curve fast, right in behind him, running flat out, and then I noticed a funny thing. As long as I stayed right in behind him, I noticed I picked up speed and stayed right with him and my car was going faster than it had ever gone before. I could tell on the tachometer. My car wasn't turning no more than 6000 before, but when I got into this drafting position, I was turning 6800 to 7000. H'it felt like the car was plumb off the ground, floating along."

"Drafting," it was discovered at Daytona, created a vacuum behind the lead car and both cars would go faster than they normally would. Junior "hitched rides" on the Pontiacs most of the afternoon, but was still second to Bobby Johns, the lead Pontiac. Then, late in the race, Johns got into a drafting position with a fellow Pontiac that was actually one lap behind him and the vacuum got so intense that the rear window blew out of Johns' car and he spun out and crashed and Junior won.

This made Junior the Lion Killer, the Little David of stock-car racing, and his performance in the 1963 season made him even more so.

Junior raced for Chevrolet at Daytona in February, 1963, and set the all-time stock-car speed record in a hundred-mile qualifying race, 164.083 miles an hour, twenty-one miles an hour faster than Parnelli Jones's winning time at Indianapolis that year. Junior topped that at Daytona in July of 1963, qualifying at 166.005 miles per hour in a five-mile run, the fastest that anyone had ever averaged that distance in a racing car of any type. Junior's Chevrolet lasted only twenty-six laps in the Daytona 500 in 1963, however. He went out with a broken push rod. Although Chevrolet announced they were pulling out of racing at this time, Junior took his car and started out on the wildest performance in the history of stock-car racing. Chevrolet wouldn't give him a cent of backing. They wouldn't even speak to him on the telephone. Half the time he had to have his own parts made. Plymouth, Mercury, Dodge, and Ford, meantime, were pouring more money than ever into stock-car racing. Yet Junior won seven Grand National races out of the thirty-three he entered and led most others before mechanical trouble forced him out.

All the while, Junior was making record qualifying runs, year after year. In the usual type of qualifying run, a driver has the track to himself and makes two circuits, with the driver with the fastest average time getting the "pole" position for the start of the race. In a way this presents stock-car danger in its purest form. Driving a stock car does not require much handling ability, at least not as compared to Grand Prix racing, because the tracks are simple banked ovals and there is almost no shifting of gears. So qualifying becomes a test of raw nerve—of how fast a man is willing to take a curve. Many of the top drivers in competition are poor at qualifying. In effect, they are willing to calculate their risks only against the risks the other drivers are taking. Junior takes the pure risk as no other driver has ever taken it.

"Pure" risk or total risk, whichever, Indianapolis and Grand Prix drivers have seldom been willing to face the challenge of Southern stock-car drivers. A.J. Foyt, last year's winner at Indianapolis, is one exception. He has raced against the Southerners and beaten them. Parnelli Jones has tried and fared badly. Driving "Southern style" has a quality that shakes a man up. The Southerners went on a tour of Northern tracks last fall. They raced at Bridgehampton, New York, and went into the corners so hard the marshals stationed at each corner kept radioing frantically to the control booth: "They're going off the track. They're all going off the track!"

But this, Junior Johnson's last race in a Dodge, was not his day, neither for qualifying nor racing. Lorenzen took the lead early and won the 250-mile race a lap ahead of the field. Junior finished third, but was never in contention for the lead.

"Come on, Junior, do my hand—"

Two or three hundred people come out of the stands and up out of the infield and onto the track to be around Junior Johnson. Junior is signing autographs in a neat left-handed script he has. It looks like it came right out of the Locker book. The girls! Levi's, stretch pants, sneaky shorts, stretch jeans, they press into the crowd with lively narbs and try to get their hands up in front of Junior and say:

"Come on, Junior, do my hand!"

In order to do a hand, Junior has to hold the girl's hand in his right hand and then sign his name with a ballpoint on the back of her hand.

"Junior, you got to do mine, too!"

"Put it on up here."

All the girls break into . . . smiles. Junior Johnson does a hand. Ah, sweet little cigarette-ad blonde! She says: "Junior, why don't you ever call me up?"

'I'spect you get plenty of calls 'thout me."

"Oh, Junior! You call me up, you hear now?"

But also a great many older people crowd in, and they say:

"Junior, you're doing a real good job out there, you're driving real good."

"Junior, when you get in that Ford, I want to see you pass that Freddie Lorenzen, you hear now?"

"Junior, you like that Ford better than that Dodge?"

And: "Junior, here's a young man that's been waiting some time and wanting to see you—" and the man lifts up his little boy in the middle of the crowd and says: "I told you you'd see Junior Johnson. This here's Junior Johnson!"

The boy has a souvenir racing helmet on his head. He stares at Junior through a buttery face. Junior signs the program he has in his hand, and then the boy's mother says:" "Junior, I tell you right now, he's beside you all the way. He can't be moved."

And then: "Junior, I want you to meet the meanest little girl in Wilkes County."

"She don't look mean to me."

Junior keeps signing autographs and over by the pits the other kids are all over his car, the Dodge. They start pulling off the decals, the ones saying Holly Farms Poultry and Autolite and God knows whatall. They fight over the strips, the shreds of decal, as if they were totems.

All this homage to Junior Johnson lasts about forty minutes. He must be signing about 250 autographs, but he is not a happy man. By and by the crowd is thinning out, the sun is going down, wind is blowing the Coca-Cola cups around, all one can hear, mostly, is a stock-car engine starting up every now and then as somebody drives it up onto a truck or something, and Junior looks around and says: "I'd rather lead one lap and fall out of the race than stroke it and finish in the money."

"Stroking it" is driving carefully in hopes of outlasting faster and more reckless cars. The opposite of stroking it is "hard-charging." Then Junior says: "I hate to get whipped up here in Wilkes County, North Carolina."

Wilkes County, North Carolina! Who was it tried to pin the name on Wilkes County, "The bootleg capital of America"? This fellow Vance Packard. But just a minute. . . .

The night after the race Junior and his fiancée, Flossie Clark, and I went into North Wilkesboro to have dinner. Junior and Flossie came by Lowes Motel and picked me up in the dreamboat white Pontiac. Flossie is a bright, attractive woman, *saftig*, well-organized. She and Junior have been going together since they were in high school. They are going to get married as soon as Junior gets his new house built. Flossie has been doing the decor. Junior

Johnson, in the second-highest income bracket in the United States for the past five years, is moving out of his father's white frame house in Ingle Hollow at last. About three hundred yards down the road. Overlooking a lot of good green land and Anderson's grocery. Junior shows me through the house, it is almost finished, and when we get to the front door, I ask him, "How much of this land is yours?"

Junior looks around for a minute, and then back up the hill, up past his three automated chicken houses, and then down into the hollow over the pasture where his $3100 Santa Gertrudis bull is grazing, and then he says: "Everything that's green is mine."

Junior Johnson's house is going to be one of the handsomest homes in Wilkes County. Yes. And— such complicated problems of class and status. Junior is not only a legendary figure as a backwoods boy with guts who made good, he is also popular personally, he is still a good old boy, rich as he is. He is also respected for the sound and sober way he has invested his money. He also has one of the best business connections in town, Holly Farms Poultry. What complicates it is that half the county, anyway, reveres him as the greatest, most fabled night-road driver in the history of Southern bootlegging. There is hardly a living soul in the hollows who can conjure up two seconds' honest moral indignation over "the whiskey business." That is what they call it, "the whiskey business." The fact is, it has some positive political overtones, sort of like the I.R.A. in Ireland. The other half of the county—well, North Wilkesboro itself is a prosperous, good-looking town of 5,000, where a lot of hearty modern business burghers are making money the modern way, like everywhere else in the U.S.A., in things like banking, poultry processing, furniture, mirror and carpet manufacture, apple growing, and so forth and so on. And one thing these men are tired of is Wilkes County's reputation as a center of moonshining. The U.S. Alcohol and Tobacco Tax agents sit over there in Wilkesboro, right next to North Wilkesboro, year in and year out, and they have been there since God knows when, like an Institution in the land, and every day that they are there, it is like a sign saying, Moonshine County. And even that is not so *bad*—it has nothing to do with it being immoral and only a little to do with it being illegal. The real thing is, it is—raw and hillbilly. And one thing thriving modern Industry is not is hillbilly. And one thing the burghers of North Wilkesboro are not about to be is hillbilly. They have split-level homes that would knock your eyes out. Also swimming pools, white Buick Snatchwagons, flagstone *terrasse*-porches enclosed with louvered glass that opens wide in the summertime, and built-in brick barbecue pits, and they give parties where they wear Bermuda shorts and Jax stretch pants and serve rum collies and play twist and bossa nova records on the hi-fi and tell Shaggy Dog jokes about strange people ordering martinis. Moonshining . . . just a minute—the truth is, North Wilkesboro. . . .

So we are all having dinner at one of the fine new restaurants in North Wilkesboro, a place of suburban plate-glass elegance. The manager knows Junior and gives us the best table in the place and comes over and talks to Junior a while about the race. A couple of men get up and come over and get Junior's autograph to take home to their sons and so forth. Then toward the end of the meal a couple of North Wilkesboro businessmen come over ("Junior, how are you, Junior. You think you're going to like that fast-backed Ford?") and Junior introduces them to me, from *Esquire Magazine.*

"*Esquire,*" one of them says. "You're not going to do like that fellow Vance Packard did, are you?"

"Vance Packard?"

"Yeah, I think it was Vance Packard wrote it. He wrote an article and called Wilkes County the bootleg capital of America. Don't pull any of that stuff. I think it was in *American* Magazine. The bootleg capital of America. Don't pull any of that stuff on us."

I looked over at Junior and Flossie. Neither one of them said anything. They didn't even change their expressions.

Ingle Hollow! The next morning I met Junior down in Ingle Hollow at Anderson's Store. That's about fifteen miles out of North Wilkesboro on County Road No. 2400. Junior is known in a lot of Southern newspapers as "the wild man from Ronda" or "the lead-footed chicken farmer from Ronda," but Ronda is only his post-office-box address. His telephone exchange, with the Wilkes Telephone Membership Corporation, is Clingman, North Carolina, and that isn't really where he lives either. Where he lives is just Ingle Hollow, and one of the communal centers of Ingle Hollow is Anderson's Store. Anderson's is not exactly a grocery store. Out front there are two gasoline pumps under an overhanging roof. Inside there are a lot of things like a soda-pop cooler filled with ice, Coca-Colas, Nehi drinks, Dr. Pepper, Double Cola, and a gumball machine, a lot of racks of Red Man chewing tobacco, Price's potato chips, OKay peanuts, cloth hats for working outdoors in, dried sausages, cigarettes, canned goods, a little bit of meal and flour, fly swatters, and I don't know what all. Inside and outside of Anderson's there are good old boys. The young ones tend to be inside, talking, and the old ones tend to be outside, sitting under the roof by the gasoline pumps, talking. And on both sides, cars; most of them new and pastel.

Junior drives up and gets out and looks up over the door where there is a row of twelve coon tails. Junior says: "Two of them gone, ain't they?"

One of the good old boys says, "Yeah," and sighs.

A pause, and the other one says, "Somebody stole 'em."

Then the first one says, "Junior, that dog of yours ever come back?"

Junior says, "Not yet."

The second good old boy says, "You looking for her to come back?"

Junior says, "I reckon she'll come back."

The good old boy says, "I had a coon dog went off like that. They don't ever come back. I went out 'ere one day, back over yonder, and there he was, cut right from here to here. I swear if it don't look like a coon got him. Something. H'it must of turned him every way but loose."

Junior goes inside and gets a Coca-Cola and rings up the till himself, like everybody who goes into Anderson's does, it seems like. It is dead quiet in the hollow except for every now and then a car grinds over the dirt road and down the way. One coon dog missing. But he still has a lot of the black and tans, named Rock. . . .

Rock, Whitey, Red, Buster are in the pen out back of the Johnson house, the old frame house. They have scars all over their faces from fighting coons. Gypsy has one huge gash in her back from fighting something. A red rooster crosses the lawn. That's a big rooster. Shirley, one of Junior's two younger sisters, pretty girls, is out by the fence in shorts, pulling weeds. Annie May is inside the house with Mrs. Johnson. Shirley has the radio outside on the porch aimed at her, The Four Seasons! "Dawn!— ahhhh, ahhhhh, ahhhhhh!" Then a lot of electronic wheeps and lulus and a screaming disc jockey, yessss! WTOB, the Vibrant Voice of Winston-Salem, North Carolina. It sounds like station WABC in New York. Junior's mother, Mrs. Johnson, is a big, good-natured woman. She comes out and says, "Did you ever see anything like that in your life? Pullin' weeds listenin' to the radio." Junior's father, Robert Glenn Johnson, Sr.—he built this frame house about thirty-five years ago, up here where the gravel road ends and the woods starts. The road just peters out into the woods up a hill. The house has a living room, four bedrooms, and a big kitchen. The living room is full of Junior's racing trophies, and so is the piano in Shirley's room. Junior was born and raised here with his older brothers, L.P., the oldest, and Fred, and his older sister, Ruth. Over yonder, up by that house, there's a man with a mule and a little plow. That's L.P. The Johnsons still keep that old mule around to plow the vegetable gardens. And all around, on all sides like a rim, are the ridges and the woods. Well, what about those woods, where Vance Packard said the agents come stealing over the ridges and good old boys go crashing through the underbrush to get away from the still and the women start "calling the cows" up and down the hollows as the signal *they* were coming. . . .

Junior motions his hand out toward the hills and says, "I'd say nearly everybody in a fifty-mile radius of here was in the whiskey business at one time or another. When we growed up here, everybody seemed to be more or less messing with whiskey, and myself and my two brothers did quite a bit of transporting. H'it was just a business, like any other business, far as we was concerned. H'it was a matter of survival. During the Depression here, people either had to do that or starve to death. H'it wasn't no gangster type of business or nothing. They's nobody that ever messed with it here that was ever out to hurt anybody. Even if they got caught, they never tried to shoot anybody or anything like that. Getting caught and pulling time, that was just part of it. H'it was just a business, like any other business. Me and my brothers, when we went out on the road at night, h'it was just like a milk run, far as we was concerned. They was certain deliveries to be made and . . ."

A milk run—yes! Well, it was a business, all right. In fact, it was a regional industry, all up and down the Appalachian slopes. But never mind the Depression. It goes back a long way before that. The Scotch-Irish settled the mountains from Pennsylvania down to Alabama, and they have been making whiskey out there as long as anybody can remember. At first it was a simple matter of economics. The land had a low crop yield, compared to the lowlands, and even after a man struggled to grow his corn, or whatever, the cost of transporting it to the markets from down out of the hills was so great, it wasn't worth it. It was much more profitable to convert the corn into whiskey and sell that. The trouble started with the Federal Government on that score almost the moment the Republic was founded. Alexander Hamilton put a high excise tax on whiskey in 1791, almost as soon as the Constitution was ratified. The "Whiskey Rebellion" broke out in the mountains of western Pennsylvania in 1794. The farmers were mad as hell over the tax. Fifteen thousand Federal troops marched out to the mountains and suppressed them. Almost at once, however, the trouble over the whiskey tax became a symbol of something bigger. This was a general enmity between the western and eastern sections of practically every seaboard state. Part of it was political. The eastern sections tended to control the legislatures, the economy and the law courts, and the western sections felt shortchanged. Part of it was cultural. Life in the western sections was rougher. Religions, codes, and styles of life were sterner. Life in the eastern capitals seemed to give off the odor of Europe and decadence. Shays' Rebellion broke out in the Berkshire hills of western Massachusetts in 1786 in an attempt to shake off the yoke of Boston, which seemed as bad as George III's. To this day people in western Massachusetts make proposals, earnestly or with down-in-the-mouth humor, that they all ought to split off from "Boston." Whiskey—the mountain people went right on making it. Whole sections of the Appalachians were a whiskey belt, just as sections of Georgia, Alabama, and Mississippi were a cotton belt. Nobody on either side ever had any moral delusions about why the Federal Government was against it. It was always the tax, pure and simple. Today the price of liquor is sixty-percent tax. Today, of course, with everybody gone wild over the subject of science and health, it has been much easier for the Federals to persuade people that they crack down on moonshine whiskey because it is dangerous, it poisons, kills, and blinds people. The statistics are usually specious.

Moonshining was *illegal*, however, that was also the unvarnished truth. And that had a side effect in the whiskey belt. The people there were already isolated, geographically, by the mountains and had strong clan ties because they were all from the same stock, Scotch-Irish. Moonshining isolated them even more. They always had to be careful who came up there. There are plenty of hollows to this day where if you drive in and ask some good old boy where so-and-so is, he'll tell you he never heard of the fellow. Then the next minute, if you identify yourself and give some idea of why you want to see him, and he believes you, he'll suddenly say, "Aw, you're talking about *so-and-so.* I thought you said—" With all this isolation, the mountain people began to take on certain characteristics normally associated, by the diffident civilizations of today, with tribes. There was a strong sense of family, clan, and honor. People would cut and shoot each other up over honor. And physical courage! They were almost like Turks that way.

In the Korean War, not a very heroic performance by American soldiers generally, there were seventy-eight Medal of Honor winners. Thirty-nine of them were from the South, and practically all of the thirty-nine were from small towns in or near the Appalachians. The New York metropolitan area, which has more people than all these towns put together, had three Medal of Honor winners, and one of them had just moved to New York from the Appalachian region of West Virginia. Three of the Medal of Honor winners came from within fifty miles of Junior Johnson's side porch.

Detroit has discovered these pockets of courage, almost like a natural resource, in the form of Junior Johnson and about twenty other drivers. There is something exquisitely ironic about it. Detroit is now engaged in the highly sophisticated business of offering the illusion of Speed for Everyman—making their cars go 175 miles an hour on racetracks—by discovering and putting behind the wheel a breed of mountain men who are living vestiges of a degree of physical courage that became extinct in most other sections of the country by 1900. Of course, very few stock-car drivers have ever had anything to do with the whiskey business. A great many always lead quiet lives off the track. But it is the same strong people among whom the whiskey business developed who produced the kind of men who could drive the stock cars. There are a few exceptions, Freddie Lorenzen, from Elmburst,

Illinois, being the most notable. But, by and large, it is the rural Southern code of honor and courage that has produced these, the most daring men in sports.

Cars and bravery! The mountain-still operators had been running white liquor with hopped-up automobiles all during the Thirties. But it was during the war that the business was so hot out of Wilkes County, down to Charlotte, High Point, Greensboro, Winston-Salem, Salisbury, places like that; a night's run, by one car, would bring anywhere from $500 to $1000. People had money all of a sudden. One car could carry twenty-two to twenty-five cases of white liquor. There were twelve half-gallon fruit jars full per case, so each load would have 132 gallons or more. It would sell to the distributor in the city for about ten dollars a gallon, when the market was good, of which the driver would get two dollars, as much as $300 for the night's work.

The usual arrangement in the white liquor industry was for the elders to design the distillery, supervise the formulas and the whole distilling process and take care of the business end of the operation. The young men did the heavy work, carrying the copper and other heavy goods out into the woods, building the still, hauling in fuel—and driving. Junior and his older brothers, L.P. and Fred, worked that way with their father, Robert Glenn Johnson, Sr.

Johnson, Senior, was one of the biggest individual copper-still operators in the area. The fourth time he was arrested, the agents found a small fortune in working corn mash bubbling in the vats.

"My Daddy was always a hard worker," Junior is telling me. "He always wanted something a little bit better. A lot of people resented that and held that against him, but what he got, he always got h'it by hard work. There ain't no harder work in the world than making whiskey. I don't know of any other business that compels you to get up at all times of night and go outdoors in the snow and everything else and work. H'it's the hardest way in the world to make a living, and I don't think anybody'd do it unless they had to."

Working mash wouldn't wait for a man. It started coming to a head when it got ready to and a man had to be there to take it off, out there in the woods, in the brush, in the brambles, in the muck, in the snow. Wouldn't it have been something if you could have just set it all up inside a good old shed with a corrugated metal roof and order those parts like you want them and not have to smuggle all that copper and all that sugar and all that everything out here in the woods and be a coppersmith and a plumber and a cooper and a carpenter and a pack horse and every other goddamned thing God ever saw in this world, all at once.

And live decent hours—Junior and his brothers, about two o'clock in the morning they'd head out to the stash, the place where the liquor was hidden after it was made. Sometimes it would be somebody's house or an old shed or some place just out in the woods, and they'd make their arrangements out there, what the route was and who was getting how much liquor. There wasn't anything ever written down. Everything was cash on the spot. Different drivers liked to make the run at different times, but Junior and his brothers always liked to start out from 3 to 4 a.m. But it got so no matter when you started out you didn't have those roads to yourself.

"Some guys liked one time and some guys liked another time," Junior is saying, "but starting about midnight they'd be coming out of the woods from every direction. Some nights the whole road was full of bootleggers. It got so some nights they'd be somebody following you going just as fast as you were and you didn't know who h'it was, the law or somebody else hauling whiskey."

And it was just a business, like any other business, just like a milk route—but this funny thing was happening. In those wild-ass times, with the money flush and good old boys from all over the county running that white liquor down the road ninety miles an hour and more than that if you try to crowd them a little bit—well, the funny thing was, it got to be competitive in an almost aesthetic, a pure sporting way. The way the good old boys got to hopping up their automobiles—it got to be a science practically. Everybody was looking to build a car faster than anybody ever had before. They practically got into industrial espionage over it. They'd come up behind one another on those wild-ass nights on the highway, roaring through the black gulches between the clay cuts and the trees, pretending like they were officers, just to challenge them, test them out, race . . . *pour le sport*, careening through the darkness, old Carolina moon. All these cars were registered in phony names. If a man had to abandon one, they would find license plates that traced back to . . . nobody at all. It wasn't anything, particularly, to go down to the Motor Vehicle Bureau and get some license plates, as long as you paid your money. Of course, it's rougher now, with compulsory insurance. You have to have your insurance before you can get your license plates, and that leads to a lot of complications. Junior doesn't know what they do about that now. Anyway, all these cars with the magnificent engines were plain on the outside, so they wouldn't attract attention, but they couldn't disguise them altogether. They were jacked up a little in the back and had 8.00 or 8.20 tires, for the heavy loads, and the sound—

"They wasn't no way you could make it sound like an ordinary car," says Junior.

God-almighty, that sound in the middle of the night, groaning, roaring, humming down into the hollows, through the clay gulches—yes! And all over the rural South, hell, all over the South, the legends of wild-driving whiskey running got started. And it wasn't just the plain excitement of it. It was something deeper, the symbolism. It brought into a modern focus the whole business, one and a half centuries old, of the country people's rebellion against the Federals, against the seaboard establishment, their independence, their defiance of the outside world. And it was like a mythology for that and for something else that was happening, the whole wild thing of the car as the symbol of liberation in the postwar South.

"They was out about every night, patrolling, the agents and the State Police was," Junior is saying, "but they seldom caught anybody. H'it was like the dogs chasing the fox. The dogs can't catch a fox, he'll just take 'em around in a circle all night long. I was never caught for transporting. We never lost but one car and the axle broke on h'it."

The fox and the dogs! Whiskey running certainly had a crazy gamelike quality about it, considering that a boy might be sent up for two years or more if he were caught transporting. But these boys were just wild enough for that. There got to be a code about the chase. In Wilkes County nobody, neither the good old boys nor the agents, ever did anything that was going to hurt the other side physically. There was supposed to be some parts of the South where the boys used smoke screens and tack buckets. They had attachments in the rear of the cars, and if the agents got too close they would let loose a smoke screen to blind them or a slew of tacks to make them blow a tire. But nobody in Wilkes County ever did that because that was a good way for somebody to get killed. Part of it was that whenever an agent did get killed in the South, whole hordes of agents would come in from Washington and pretty soon they would be tramping along the ridges practically inch by inch, smoking out the stills. But mainly it was—well, the code. If you got caught, you went along peaceably, and the agents never used their guns. There were some tense times. Once was when the agents started using tack belts in Ardell County. This was a long strip of leather studded with nails that the agents would lay across the road in the dark. A man couldn't see it until it was too late and he stood a good chance of getting killed if it got his tires and spun him out. The other was the time the State Police put a roadblock down there at that damned bridge at Millersville to catch a couple of escaped convicts. Well, a couple of good old boys rode up with a load, and there was the roadblock and they were already on the bridge, so they jumped out and dove into the water. The police saw two men jump out of their car and dive in the water, so they opened fire and they shot one good old boy in the backside. As they pulled him out, he kept saying:

"What did you have to shoot at me for? What did you have to shoot at me for?"

It wasn't pain, it wasn't anguish, it wasn't anger. It was consternation. The bastards had broken the code.

Then the Federals started getting radio cars.

"The radios didn't do them any good," Junior says. "As soon as the officers got radios, then *they* got radios. They'd go out and get the same radio. H'it was an awful hard thing for them to radio them down. They'd just listen in on the radio and see where they're setting up the roadblocks and go a different way."

And such different ways. The good old boys knew back roads, dirt roads, up people's back lanes and every which way, and an agent would have to live in the North Carolina hills a lifetime to get to know them. There wasn't hardly a stretch of road on any of the routes where a good old boy couldn't duck off the road and into the backcountry if he had to. They had wild detours around practically every town and every intersection in the region. And for tight spots—the legendary devices, the "bootleg slide," the siren and the red light. . . .

And then one day in 1955 some agents snuck over the ridges and caught Junior Johnson at his daddy's still. Junior Johnson, the man couldn't *any-body* catch!

The arrest caught Junior just as he was ready to really take off in his career as a stock-car driver. Junior says he hadn't been in the whiskey business in any shape or form, hadn't run a load of whiskey for two or three years, when he was arrested. He was sentenced to two years in the Federal reformatory in Chillicothe, Ohio.

"If the law felt I should have gone to jail, that's fine and dandy," Junior tells me. "But I don't think the true facts of the case justified the sentence I got. I never had been arrested in my life. I think they was punishing me for the past. People get a kick out of it because the officers can't catch somebody, and this angers them. Soon as I started getting publicity for racing, they started making it real hot for my family. I was out of the whiskey business, and they knew that, but they was just waiting to catch me on something. I got out after serving ten months and three days of the sentence, but h'it was two or three years I was set back, about half of '56 and every bit of '57. H'it takes a year to really get back into h'it after something like that. I think I lost the prime of my racing career."

But, if anything, the arrest only made the Junior Johnson legend hotter.

And all the while Detroit kept edging the speeds up, from 150 m.p.h. in 1960 to 155 to 165 to 175 to 180 flat out on the longest straightaway, and the good old boys of Southern stock-car racing stuck right with it. Any speed Detroit would give them they would take right with them into the curve, hard-charging even though they began to feel strange things such as the rubber starting to pull right off the tire casing. And God! Good old boys from all over the South roared together after the Stanchion-Speed! Guts!—pouring into Birmingham, Daytona Beach, Randleman, North Carolina; Spartanburg, South Carolina; Weaverville, Hillsboro, North Carolina; Atlanta, Hickory, Bristol, Tennessee; Augusta, Georgia; Richmond, Virginia; Asheville, North Carolina; Charlotte, Myrtle Beach— tens of thousands of them. And still upper- and middle-class America, even in the South, keeps its eyes averted. Who cares! They kept on heading out where we all live, after all . . . even outside a town like Darlington, a town of 10,000 souls, God, here they come, down Route 52, up 401, on 340, 151 and 34, on through the South Carolina mesas. By Friday night already the good old boys are pulling into the infield of the Darlington raceway with those blazing pastel dreamboats stacked this way and that on the clay flat and the Thermos jugs and the brown whiskey bottles coming on out. By Sunday—the race!—there are 65,000 piled into the racetrack at

Darlington. The sheriff, as always, sets up the jail right there in the infield. No use trying to haul them out of there. And now—the *sound* rises up inside the raceway, and a good old boy named Ralph goes mad and starts selling chances on his Dodge. Twenty-five cents and you can take the sledge he has and smash his car anywhere you want. How they roar when the windshield breaks! The police could interfere, you know, but they are busy chasing a good old girl who is playing Lady Godiva on a hog-backed motorcycle, naked as sin, hauling around and in and out of the clay ruts.

Eyes averted, happy burghers. On Monday the ads start appearing—for Ford, for Plymouth, for Dodge—announcing that we gave it to you, speed such as you never saw. There it was! At Darlington, Daytona, Atlanta—and not merely in the Southern papers but in the albino pages of the suburban women's magazines, such as *The New Yorker*, in color— the Ford winners, such as Fireball Roberts, grinning with a cigar in his mouth in *The New Yorker*. And somewhere, some Monday morning, Jim Paschal of High Point, Ned Jarrett of Boykin, Cale Yarborough of Timmonsville and Curtis Crider from Charlotte, Bobby Isaac of Catawba, E.J. Trivette of Deep Gap, Richard Petty of Randleman, Tiny Lund of Cross, South Carolina; Stick Elliott of Shelby—and from out of Ingle Hollow.

And all the while, standing by in full Shy, in Alumicron suits—there is Detroit, hardly able to believe itself, what it has discovered, a breed of good old boys from the fastnesses of the Appalachian hills and flats—a handful from this rare breed—who have given Detroit . . . speed . . . and the industry can present it to a whole generation as . . . yours. And the Detroit P.R. men themselves come to the tracks like folk worshipers and the millions go giddy with the thrill of speed. Only Junior Johnson goes about it as if it were . . . the usual. Junior goes on down to Atlanta for the Dixie 400 and drops by the Federal penitentiary to see his Daddy. His Daddy is in on his fifth illegal distillery conviction; in the whiskey business that's just part of it; an able craftsman, an able businessman, and the law kept hounding him, that was all. So Junior drops by and then goes on out to the track and gets in his new Ford and sets the qualifying speed record for Atlanta Dixie 400, 146.301 m.p.h.; later on he tools on back up the road to Ingle Hollow to tend to the automatic chicken houses and the road-grading operation. Yes.

Yet how can you tell that to . . . anybody . . . out on the bottom of that bowl as the motor thunder begins to lift up through him like a sigh and his eyeballs glaze over and his hands reach up and there, riding the rim of the bowl, soaring over the ridges, is Junior's yellow Ford . . . which is his white Chevrolet . . . which is a White Ghost, forever rousing the good old boys . . . hard-charging! . . . up with the automobile into their America, and the hell with arteriosclerotic old boys trying to hold onto the whole pot with arms of cotton seersucker. Junior!

Contributor Biographies

Adrian Blevins is the author of two books of poetry as well as two chapbooks. She is also a recipient of the Lamar York prize in nonfiction.

Greg Bottoms is the author of seven books of creative nonfiction and fiction, including the memoir *Angelhead*. He teaches creative writing at the University of Vermont, where he is a Professor of English.

Michael P. Branch, Professor of English at the University of Nevada-Reno, has published five books and more than two hundred essays, articles, and reviews.

Kelly Cherry is the author or translator of over thirty books in multiple genres, including *A Kelly Cherry Reader.*

Michael Chitwood has published eight books of poetry and two collections of nonfiction.

Casey Clabough is the author of eleven books, including *The Warrior's Path* and its sequel-in-part *The End of the Mountains.*

Mark Edmundson is the author of eleven books of nonfiction, including works on athletics, education, gothicism, literature, philosophy, psychoanalysis, and rock and roll.

Margaret Gibson is the author of eleven books of poetry. An altered version of "Queen of Hearts" later appeared in her memoir *The Prodigal Daughter: Reclaiming an Unfinished Childhood.*

John Pineda is the author of two poetry collections, a novel, and the memoir *Sleep in Me.*

Lucinda Roy is the author of five books, including *No Right to Remain Silent.*

Matthew Vollmer is the author or editor of six books, including the essay collection *Inscriptions for Headstones.*

Tom Wolfe is widely recognized for his influence on the development of American New Journalism and Creative Nonfiction. He is the author of fifteen books.